MW00619398

being my first NYC friend! Love you always ♡ Hope

30 THINGS
BEFORE 30

Hope Alcocer

30 Things Before 30

Copyright © 2018 by Hope Alcocer

All rights reserved. No part of this book may be reproduced or transmitted in any form or by any means without written permission of the author.

ISBN 978-0-692-05895-4

Contents

Foreword i

1   Never Beg for Love. 1

2   It's Not about the Pounds. 6

3   Shut Up and Stop Complaining 19

4   Use Your Voice. 26

5   You Don't Have to Swallow 32

6   You Only Need Three Things to Live
    (and it's Not Him) 37

7   Not Everybody Is a Photographer
    (The it Factor) 39

8   If He Says He's Not Like Every Other Guy,
    Then He Is Exactly Like Every Other Guy 43

9   Getting Married Is Not the Be-All-End-All . . . 52

10 Your Parents Did the Best They Could 58

11 Abuse is Abuse 61

12 Stop Saying Yes 64

13 College Isn't for Everyone 68

14 Mental Health Is a Thing 74

15 A Leopard Doesn't Change It's Spots 81

16 Find a Mentor 84

17 Nobody Cares 90

18 Be Selfish 93

19 Adopt Self-Care 97

20 Set Boundaries 101

21 Collaborate, Don't Compete 104

22 Make Time to See your Grandparents 108

23 Stay Current 114

24 Social Media is a Lie 119

25 Cut the Cord 126

26 You Don't Owe Anyone an Explanation 133

27 It's Quality Over Quantity 139

28 Not Everyone Is Going to Like You 146

29 Stop Being So Readily Available 152

30 You're Failing If You're Not Even Trying 159

Foreword

Growing up I was a very protective big sister of my younger sister and brother.

I felt the need to supervise everything they did, comment on every move they made, and at the end of the day, I needed to know everybody was tucked in safe and sound. If someone was sick, I had to make sure I was checking on them, monitoring them as though it was 1822 and typhoid fever was a thing again.

Mind you, we had competent and loving parents, so I'm not too sure where my need to be the watchdog off of 101 Dalmatians stemmed from.

As they grew older, they were naturally immersed in situations and allotted experiences that I had once gone through. Some were joyous and triumphant; others led to heartache, disappointment, and discouragement. And each time they hurt, I hurt. "You should have listened to me!" I'd exclaim. "I did it wrong this one time, and this happened! Why didn't you learn from my mistakes?" "You wouldn't hurt as much."

It wasn't about a need to be right, or a need for them to do it my way. It wasn't about ego or being the bossy know-it-all big sister. I just hated seeing my siblings hurt. See, I had the notion, if they had just done it a different way, a way I wish I would have, perhaps they wouldn't be hurting as bad. I still do that to this day. However, they're both in their 20s, and they let me know in a plethora of ways that my big sister sarcastic opinion or "now what did we learn from this" styled overview isn't always the best way to love on them. I'll work on it for the second half of our lives, sibs.

This book is a conglomerate of lessons learned over the last couple decades. Most of them are lessons and takeaways I've discovered after being hurt, or badly burnt, or sent back to the START square on this game board we call life. This book is written with the best of intentions, and all of you in my heart and mind.

If I can spare any woman anywhere in the world an ounce of heartache, difficulty, or confusion, if I can save them a couple of moments of their precious time, then my struggle was worth it.

If I can share the wisdom I have gleaned so that my readers don't have to take the rocky detours I had to, then my growing pains and my 'WTF' moments were worth something.

Please, bear in mind, just because there is a chapter written about a particular concept, it does not mean I've nailed the million dollar secret. I'm a work in progress, and I struggle daily. I am still seeking answers, and I am still working on several of these topics discussed in this book. I'm still meeting with my therapist -- weekly. I swear off men-- monthly. I try and embrace my body, mind, and soul-- daily.

Girl- if I can do it, I know you can do it too.

All my love,
XO Hope

Chapter 1.
Never Beg for Love

THERE WAS A time when I would have given every fiber of my being—mind, body, heart, and soul—to keep the person with whom I wanted to spend the rest of my life. Once, I stood in my driveway and watched him hop into his Jeep. As he drove away, I knelt down on the pavement, sobbing, begging him to not leave.

But he wasn't there to hear me.

Days and nights passed as I stared at my phone, hoping that it would light up and make the "pop!" sound of an incoming text. I longed for the text to be from him, telling me that he wanted to take it all back.

At the lowest point after the breakup, I just laid in bed. I lost nearly ten pounds in a week. I was starving. He had consumed me. Our playlist hummed in the background as I stared up at the ceiling. Perhaps if I prayed hard enough to whoever was up there, he would come back and say that it was all a lapse in judgment.

One day, he did return. He came back to tell me that this was it.

There he was, just a shell. A shell I loved more than I could ever put into words. I don't know how someone could have a flame that once burned so deeply for you and then have it so quickly extinguished. It felt like I was hugging a stranger as I tried to hug him hello. He didn't hug me back. His arms, limp at his sides. The look in his eyes had changed. The fire, the passion, his love for me—all gone.

Gone.

He might as well have been a sheet—a sheet of skin over organs without a soul. He had moved on. Just several weeks ago, we were preparing to be man and wife.

"Please," I begged. "Please don't go."

I will be whoever you want, I thought. Just, please, don't go. I'll be whoever you need. I'll change any fiber of my being. Just don't go.

But he went; he had to. He wasn't happy. He had fallen out of love, and I would not be able to change his mind.

I begged, I bargained. But he had checked out long ago.

The day that he left for good, I crawled onto my bed and stayed. I didn't eat or drink, and I just cried harder than I think I ever had before. I mourned what I thought we were, and I grieved at how much I thought he loved me. I just kept dozing off, hoping I'd wake up and realize this was all just a bad dream.

I went through our messages, looking for a phrase or sentence or period that would tell me that he cared more than he let on. I switched to each social media network, looking for the last time he logged on and to see what he was liking or commenting on. I was just looking for a sign that he was hurting too.

This went on for days until the days turned into a week. I'll never forget the day that I felt like I couldn't take it anymore. I was starving, but I didn't want to eat because that would have taken too much energy, and it would take away from the time that I needed to spend watching for him on social media.

Looking back, I wish I could have taken my own face in my hands and said, "Sweetie, he's not worth it." But I wasn't there yet. I wasn't mature enough for that yet. I'll never forget the day that I couldn't take it anymore. My bedroom, at the time, had two floors of stairs leading up to it. My mom came up to me and said, "Sweetie, it's time to start healing." And I'll never forget being so angry at her. Who was she to tell me when it's time? And I said, "I'm not ready yet. He's coming back; he's coming back."

My mom looked me in the eyes and said, "If he comes back, then he comes back. Hope, you should never beg for love. You are worth something. You are worth something in the eyes of me. You are worth something in the eyes of your family. And you are worth something in the eyes of your friends and in the eyes of God. If you have to question how a man feels about you, then he does not love you like you think he does. You should never have to beg for love, and if someone truly loves you, you should never have to overanalyze every thought, every movement, every text, every word, every tone—because you just know they love you. And above all, my daughter should never beg for love."

You should never beg someone to love you; it should be something that someone is honored to do, whether they've been with you for a year, two years, or five years. If they truly felt the way that they claimed they did on social media and to friends and family, then it should never be called into question. And while you may not be dealing with this exact situation, I put this lesson first in the book because I want this to light a fire under your soul.

We do not need to beg and borrow and overanalyze and ask for a committee of our girlfriends to help us figure out how someone truly feels by the way that they text us—did they include an emoji? Did they capitalize that word? Did they include an exclamation mark? If someone truly cares about you, beyond a shadow of a doubt, you should not have to beg for their attention. You should not have to look for it or seek it. It should be there.

And if you are in a relationship where you have to beg, bargain, or overanalyze, then you are in the wrong relationship. You are a human, a person. You should never question a man or a woman's affection for you, and you should never question a man or woman's opinion of you. It should be evident. It should be communicated day after day because you are not a prize to be won. When someone chooses to love you, it should be evident in every action, thought, and conversation.

My darling, you are a star. You are a bombshell. You are a bad ass, and there is no scenario in which you should beg for someone's love. Period.

Chapter 2.
It's Not about the Pounds

WHEN YOU GLANCED at this title, you were probably thinking: Oh, oh, another chapter about loving yourself exactly how you are. It doesn't matter if you're eight hundred pounds—you're still beautiful. Yadda, yadda, yadda.

Wrong.

I mean, that's sort of right.

I am going to tell you to love yourself. I'll also tell you to love yourself where you're at. Yeah, also that you're beautiful, even if you're eight hundred pounds.

But first, you need to understand that it's not about the pounds. Now, this is a delicate topic because it does matter if you're healthy. But as long as you acknowledge that you need to be healthy, you can still love and embrace yourself. That being said, the number on the scale does not matter.

As long as you like to look in the mirror and not talk down to yourself, then, in my opinion, the number on the scale doesn't matter. Enjoy having sex with the lights on. Dance naked when you get ready in the morning. Wear clothes that make you feel sexy. Be proud of yourself. Whether you're two hundred or one hundred seven pounds, flaunt what you've got.

As women, we're biologically meant to have children—that is, if you choose to want little screaming parasites one day. But whether or not you choose to take action and procreate, you cannot deny that we are designed to bear little ones. Our body was ergonomically designed to do so. I was reminded of this as I sat down at the table to write this chapter and my butt and thighs were served with the avocado toast at the table next to me as I tried to squeeze my way into this tiny booth. Anyway, with pregnancy and childbirth comes a tradeoff—hormones. And with hormone fluctuation comes weight fluctuation. Weight fluctuation is a part of being human, especially a part of being a woman, but it can often lead to feelings of abnormality. You'll think: Am I the ideal weight? But, to figure this out, you must factor in various conditions. Genetics, lifestyle, activity level, other health issues, even down to when you eat your meals each day.

It has taken me twenty-five years to figure this out. I am thirty years old. I'm not explaining this in the best possible way I can, so I'm going to start out by telling you my story of body image and self-love. It's not a story

I like to tell. It's pretty embarrassing, many parts of it. But through every lesson and trial and tribulation, I have learned that if I can't share it and you can't take a piece of it, then my pain and struggle was all for nothing.

My story begins when I am five years old, picture little Hopie so excited because guess where we're going today? Dance class, and not just any dance class, but ballet. I'm five years old. I have this curly, little afro and super dark skin that made everyone wonder my ethnicity as it seemed doubtful I was Armenian and Spanish. I looked like Beyoncé's kid.

It was the first day of class, and I was like, "Mom, let's go get ready," probably four hours before the class even started. She's helping me get ready, and I'm wriggling into my tights. I wasn't fat, but I remember my mom helping me get my little chunky thighs into the tights and the dance leotard. I remember her telling me "you are adorable." Uh duh, yah mom, I know.

I'm Armenian and Latina, and when you mix the two together, you get a hell of a lot of curves, a lot of passion, attitude, and you have a hard time fitting into your dance leotard.

At the time, I was dealing with a digestion issue. I swallowed a lot of air at meals because I ate so fast. Again, I'm Armenian and Latin. We live to eat, not eat to live. Food is our thing. I already had a bloated belly from filling up like an air balloon. They called me Buddha—Buddha belly.

So I'm trying to fit this dance leotard over my Buddha belly, and I'm like, "Mom, it's not fitting." She's helping me adjust it. At the time, perhaps I thought that it was a bit funny. I have a picture to remember the moment. I wasn't self-conscious then. I didn't even think twice that maybe something's wrong with me or perhaps I'm not normal, or maybe I'm not going to be as skinny as all of the girls in my class.

We're ready to go to dance class, right? When we get there, everybody has pink tights like me. Everybody has black dance leotards like me. Everybody has their hair in a ballerina bun like me. Some have cool hair like I do, but no one looks like Buddha. I was so happy to be in class, despite the fact that I didn't dance very well. I wasn't athletic back then, and I'm still not athletic, but I was so excited to be there. I wore that dance leotard every day. Even if I wasn't at dance class, I would put on my dance leotard after dinner and pull it over my little Buddha belly.

And then it started.

Little kids—my peers—would poke my stomach and ask if I was pregnant, or they would tell me that I was fat. I'd ask, "Mom, what's wrong with me? Why are people laughing at my tummy?" And she'd always say, "You're fine. You're perfect. You're beautiful. They don't understand. You're perfect. Everybody has a little belly. It's normal. It's fine."

One day, I got stung by a wasp. I was pretending to play soccer for my mom's sake. Sometimes I just sat there like a bump on a log (my mom used this expression, so I just assume it means lazy) and stared at the ball, and sometimes I liked to pick the dandelions and stick them behind my ear. Very athletic.

But one day a wasp got into my shirt and bit my stomach. After I went to the nurse, she gave me liquid Benadryl to continue dabbing on my stomach as the day proceeded. I walked around with my shirt up and poked curiously at the wound, little hypochondriac that I was. But even with an injury, the remarks still flooded my ears.

You're fat. You're pregnant. Are you going to have a babyyyyy?

Seriously, third graders can be fucking assholes.

My insecurities blossomed like the dandelions that I used to enjoy picking while my self-esteem eroded.

I bit my little cheek and started to wonder if they were right.

There was nothing for me to cling onto as I tumbled down the slippery slope and landed in a pile of shit. I despised myself.

As time went on, I noticed that I didn't look like other girls. My mom used to watch All My Children. I don't remember when it was on, but she would watch it. I'd sneak in and look at these gorgeous women with all of their man-drama, and I vowed that I would one day have a life that dramatic. But I realized that I didn't look like them.

I remember wondering what was wrong with me. I'd try to suck in my stomach, or I would wear baggy clothes to hide my Buddha belly. I started exercising. By exercise, I mean that I ran back and forth in my yard until I was out of breath. Or I walked up and down the stairs three times, and I was good. Cardio? Check.

Once the initial bullying and teasing started, it was a slippery slope of self-doubt and self-loathing. I wanted to be like the other girls. When I started playing with my Barbie dolls, I was intensely aware that they all had thigh gaps, toned stomachs, firm boobs, and they were perfect to me. I was obsessed. I began to seek out every beautiful girl that I could find—in school, on posters, on the street, in the store—and admire her from afar, envy her voluptuous body.

No one told me what I was doing wrong. I would eat out of boredom, all the time. My mom didn't advise me on how to tone my body or eat healthier, for fear I would become obsessive about food intake. In the meantime, I kept throwing back food like I was getting paid for it—too much baklava, too many cookies, and too many scoops of popcorn.

I reached puberty. With no assistance and the remarks still pouring in like I was a restaurant being reviewed and my customers had all been served poison, I reached the point where I said, "Fuck it. Nothing's working. I'm just going to start binge eating." I became homeschooled during this time, but it wasn't for me.

Don't even get me started on that. My mom put my siblings and me in this homeschool co-op so that we could have "socialization" because, in 1999, that was a big deal. Everyone's freaking out that these homeschoolers wouldn't get enough socialization. I digress. My mom signed me up for a sports team. I was on the volleyball team. Let me tell you about my journey on the volleyball team. We had two teams. We had an A team and a B team, okay? I was on the B team. I also never played a game. That's how good I was at volleyball.

However, I was fantastic at getting rid of candy bars for our fundraisers. Sometimes I used my birthday money just to buy myself an entire box of candy. Particularly ones with the Cadbury caramel center. I gutted the entire box within a month. I'd go to the bathroom just to eat the candy bars and then flush down the wrappers.

I thought: Nothing is changing about my body. I'm still fat, all these years later. I still have this belly and flabby thighs. No one's even seen me on the team. No one lets me play. I don't have a ton of friends. So what's the point of trying? What's the point of trying to get thin or slimming myself or losing weight or exercising? If nothing's changing, I'm just going to keep eating because eating feels good.

And so I did just that.

Being conservative, I was twenty to twenty-five pounds heavier than I should have been from ages twelve until my early 20s. But as a child all the way through my teen years, my mom never said anything. I had that awesome mom who never said a word was always like, "You look beautiful. I love you." She'd encourage me to go out and play. Without any friends, I'd sit on a rock in my backyard and order my brother around.

When I went to a private high school, I sat in class with these skinny, blonde girls with their blue or green eyes and size two to four bodies. It was 2004, so they had their hair flipped out and highlighted because highlighting using a cap was cool then. Dressed head to toe in Abercrombie, American Eagle, and Hollister. Those brands were made for those body types: perky tits, hourglass stomachs, and sharp hips.

Oh, look, I don't fit in again. I look nothing like these girls.

The round-assed, brown-skinned girl, wearing a size eight.

When the college years rolled around, I started skipping meals. Hey, if I skipped a meal, I wouldn't bloat. My stomach didn't look quite as big the next day. Or if I skipped a couple of meals, my face would look a little thinner. I didn't partake in this regularly, but it was my own experiment. I was also involved in dance throughout college, and those childhood demons crept back in all over again. Classes and dance practices full of those types of girls all over again, it was impossible to escape this obsession with getting thin.

I had a very rough time in college for multiple reasons, one of which being dealing with a head injury. My family, low life boyfriend, and health issues made me grit my teeth from bitterness. I had been screwed out of all of the control in my life, so I decided to grip my weight with an even tighter fist. I skipped all three meals. The next day, five pounds disappeared. I was obsessed with losing weight, and losing weight the incorrect and unhealthy way.

I got involved in a vicious cycle.

This issue crept in and out of my life until fast forward, I was twenty-five years old and happily engaged to a fitness guru. My fiancée, at the time, was into fitness as well, so it just indirectly fed into this illness I was developing without even realizing it. I got down to one hundred fifteen pounds and had never felt better about myself.

Laxatives and diuretics led to me losing five to seven pounds per week. During the period of time in which my engagement was nearing an end, I weighed one hundred ten pounds. I didn't have enough strength to even hold myself up in the shower. Because of how I had gone about losing the weight—becoming dehydrated and depriving myself of nutrients—I was as thin as a waif. I had so many people coming to me and saying, "What is wrong with you? Are you okay? Do you need any help? Are you sick?" I'd get defensive. By the grace of God, I eventually snapped out of it. But then the cycle continued. After my fiancé left, I went on a literal cupcake binge. I gained about forty pounds back. That's another story for another day.

That was almost five years ago. I'm giving you the synopsis of my weight, self-love, and body journey. It has been the source of my depression, anxiety, and tears for as many years as I can remember. It is crazy to think how your self-esteem can be completely taken down just by looking at someone skinnier than you. It is beyond belief, the guilt that you can feel from eating a cheeseburger. It's insane to me that we run past the mirror because we don't want to look at ourselves. It's so sad to me that we want to have sex with the lights off because we're afraid that our stomach is going to be too noticeable.

Here's the thing. I weigh, as of right now, one hundred thirty pounds, but I'm healthy. I am made of muscle. I have a peach-emoji ass. I used to be so obsessed with the number on the scale, but it's taken me almost twenty-five years to learn that it's not about the scale. We need to love ourselves exactly where we are. And if your figure does mean something to you, then remember there are healthy things to do to control our weight, and that means eating right, exercising, and watching your portions. I don't mean being obsessed with it, but we can work out and completely cancel out what we did by not eating correctly. Stick to your goals and love yourself in the meantime.

There's this huge controversy about weight and loving people—like fat love. People who are overweight are just as beautiful and wonderful as people who are slender. And I'm absolutely floored that people who are naturally skinny are getting skinny shamed as well. What the hell is that about? It shouldn't be the number on the scale that concerns you. It's a question of: are you healthy—physically, mentally, emotionally to be able to live your life as the best version of you? You should be healthy enough to live a long and happy life. Studies show that being obese will shorten your life. Studies also show that being too thin can be detrimental to your health. You could have cardio issues if you are too fat or too thin. You could potentially have hormonal issues if you are under or overweight. Extreme weight loss or gain can lead to low libido, low energy, or missed periods. But it is not about the pounds. Everybody has their own personal, individual standard of what is normal based on so many factors. And that, my love, is something that should only be determined by a health professional. Not your friend who has a cool fitness Instagram page. Not a blog article. A trained health professional. Because your standard of healthy is not the person's next to you. So, first figure that out. Once you get that down with the help of a doctor or a trained professional, who cares if you could technically lose ten pounds? Who cares if you have cellulite? Who cares if you have a little pudge that goes over your yoga pants? Who cares if when you're having crazy, wild, passionate sex, and your tummy is bloated and jiggling a bit. There's more of you to love than just your outer appearance. This is where you pretend I'm pointing to your heart, and then we hug and go eat guacamole.

It's also about a level of acceptance. It's about understanding your body. Maybe you have hormonal issues or a chronic illness that has caused you to gain fifteen pounds that you just can't seem to shed. Maybe you're pregnant. Maybe you already had the baby, and you can't seem to get rid of the post-baby weight. Love yourself. Be patient. Give yourself time to work toward a shape with which you are comfortable, and then learn to love yourself in the skin that you have.

Learn to be okay with weight fluctuation. If the stock market can rise and fall, so can your weight from time to time. You may be one size one week and another the next. Do not obsess about it. That does absolutely nothing. Maybe you don't want to exercise one week. Maybe you want to smash a cheeseburger instead. So fucking what. Do it. It's good to indulge sometimes. Take some time to date yourself and figure out what dietary lifestyle works best for you. It is not about the number on the scale. For me, a good measure of where I'm at with this is if I can look in the mirror without running past, if I can have sex with the lights kinda on (thank GOD for dimmers), or if I can strut proudly in a great pair of pumps and skinny jeans. Things like that.

Are you happy with yourself? Do you feel good? Do you feel healthy? Then, in my book (literally), you are at optimal weight. Because in this situation, optimal weight means that you have started to love yourself. You should be proud of yourself. It's not about the pounds. Love your body. Love yourself.

If you keep this mantra, your body will reward you. Your body knows when you loathe yourself, so I encourage you to start reframing your mind. Try to get rid of that negativity. You will be amazed at the results you see.

Chapter 3.
Shut Up and Stop Complaining

HI. JUST MAKING sure you're still with me. That last one was a rant. I'll never write about anything unless I, too, have been the student of that lesson or topic I'm writing about. If you can learn something from my stories, struggles and preachy moments, then I have succeeded. That's important. I can't be any more real with you. I'm baring it all, and you must bear with me as I tell you about this next part of my life.

Like everyone, I get unmotivated. But this particular period of time was my last year of college when everyone else is finding internships and renting apartments. My mom said to me, ever-so-kindly: "Hope, okay, you're about to finish school. What are you going to do with your life? Like, you need to … are you going … you know, you know, you can't live with us. I mean, you can, but only for a certain period of time. What are you going to do with your life? Like, how are you going to move out? What is your plan?"

"Well, I don't have one, Mom."

"Okay, you need to get moving. You need to get your ducks in a row."

It was the first time, in twenty-something years of life, that I did not know what I was doing. I think that's most almost college graduates, though. I just sort of sat in it, though. And complained. I was in a very negative state of affairs at that phase in my life.

I would complain about my health. I would complain about my weight. I would complain about my boyfriend. I would complain about my degree program. I would complain about where I lived. I would complain about my apartment. I would complain about my future.

You get the point.

One day, my mom and I had a heart-to-heart. Dad was sitting alongside during this conversation. He can be a brilliant man of few words. He'll put in a word here or there, and it reminds me of Yoda, the blue-assed monkey from The Lion King, Buddha, and Grandmother Willow from Pocahontas. It's like they've all combined into this half mute parent and he'll just say five words of such in-tune, insane wisdom. But then he just walks away like it never happened after dropping the metaphoric mic.

At the time that I complained every single day, I was dealing with health issues. Depression weighed on me like a leaden affliction. I had mini-seizures every single day for fourteen months. I had not been able to drive. I was turning to stone. I visited the doctor on a weekly basis. I had to be treated for my head injury. The thing that absorbed me the most was a toxic relationship that I was afraid of stepping out of, for who would have wanted someone sick and angry? So sick that she could barely manage school.

My mom once said, "Okay, so you've been complaining for about, you know, six months. What are you going to do with your life?"

I complained so much that it had become my breath.

Breathe in.

Complain.

Breathe out.

Complain.

Then came my dad's couple words of wisdom for the month. He said, "Hope, it's all in your control."

And I got really offended by that.

At the time, I didn't properly pluck my eyebrows, so I had these paper-thin eyebrows. When I warped my expression into one of disgust, I'm sure that I looked even scarier than how I imagine it right now. And I just looked at him. A spray-tanned Oompa Loompa with pencil-thin eyebrows. Spray tanning was the thing back then. Some of you might remember.

I shut him down with "Okay, Dad, thanks."

And he calmly responded, "Hope, no one is responsible for your future but you. This is all in your control."

And that was all it took to snap me out of my thing. I'm still not sure why.

I turned into the Energizer Bunny—making my own homework, trying to find the cure to cancer by mixing together Windex and mayonnaise. I was constantly on the go, being innovative and energetic. I was always trying to go, but then I hit this slump.

What the fuck do I do now?

My depression hung over me—this voluminous, bulbous cloud that wouldn't let the sunshine through.

I gained weight. I lost friends. I was miserable. Every thought ended up turning into a negative one. But what he said was true. It's all in your control.

Jim Rohn, a dead guy, once said, "You are not a tree." And when you hear that, you're like, "Yes, I know I'm not a tree." But it's so much deeper than that. You're not a tree. You don't have roots. You're not grounded. You can move. You can blossom anywhere that you're planted.

This is something that I say to my friends all the time. I've had to step away from some of them because they're so goddamn negative. I love them with all of my heart, and I would take a bullet for them, but I have a hard time being around them because everything that comes out of their mouths is so goddamn destructive. They act like they're in a headlock and unable to change their lives, make positive movements, switch their jobs, or leave their boyfriends and find a new place to live. They have excuse after excuse after excuse, and those excuses have excuses, and then you can be sure that those excuses have more excuses.

This happens so often when I go back home. I'm trying to catch up and relate to these beautiful souls that have been there through so much of high school, college, and after school. These are my people, right? These are the people with whom I wanted to grow old. I wanted to have them at my wedding as bridesmaids and eventually make playdates with them for our kids. But I'm drained by the time I step away from them.

I'm not saying to go abandoning your friends. They don't have the plague, and they aren't lesser than you. I'm telling you this because you need to make a decision about friends that boast of "Woe is me" this and "I can't change my life" that. There's no growth to be had with people like that, so when you are with them, you become stagnant. A tree. You are not supposed to be a tree.

Negativity is contagious, and that is why you need to separate yourself from it. This chapter is about learning to surround yourself with positivity, but it's also about figuring out how to shut the fuck up and stop complaining.

You are in control, even if you find yourself in a situation that you cannot control, like a debilitating illness. You control your attitude. You control your response. You control your future. We are all given the same amount of hours in a day. We were all given the fresh start of life, but then it is up to us what we choose to do with that time.

Yes, there will be elements that you can't control. If you're walking down a path and it rains, you can't stop the weather from happening. You can't control if you accidentally swallow a bug, or if someone rear ends you. Sure, you're shit out of luck when it comes to things like that, but then you can decide if you want to go inside and wait out the rain or cough up the protein-filled insect. Some horribly analogies here, but you get it, right?

I do not speak on this topic lightly. It is so difficult to climb out of the dark chasm that has become your life. It is so difficult to plow through negative thoughts and pull yourself out of the monotonous routine that has perhaps led you to gain weight or some other supposedly disastrous thing. Maybe you stopped having sex with your boyfriend, for whom you no longer have feelings. Maybe your negativity about your job has caused you to perform poorly at your job. These negative thoughts have set you up for more negative thoughts, which has, in turn, led to a negative life.

I know it looks bleak. It seems like you've been in this pattern for so long. How on God's green earth do you get out of it? Just move. Do one thing out of the ordinary. Do one thing out of your routine, even if you're too tired or don't have time to do it. Buy something healthier at the supermarket. Go to a Pilates class. Have anxiety? Feel like you can't finish a workout? Only go for twenty minutes. Work on your resume. Your resume is too overwhelming? Completely understandable. Do it little by little.

Your depression and the habits of negativity will tell you that you don't have time. They will tell you that you're not good enough. They will tell you that you're too tired. It's mind over matter. Only you can pull yourself out of this, this rut, because only you placed yourself in there.

Eventually, you will see the change. For every one positive thought, it seems like we have three negative thoughts. I'm not good at math. I've failed college math four times, but imagine how many negative thoughts that brought on. This means that we are going to have to completely retrain our minds. Basically, you'll be in a bat-shit crazy conversation with yourself, but I promise—you'll be fine.

Your body hears you. Your brain understands you. Your mind, heart, soul, spirit, cells—they listen to you. And when you put out negativity, your body adapts to that. Its innate response is to mold every thought and make them negative.

You're not going to catch every negative thought. There's going to be plenty that happens in your life to make you feel at your lowest, but I encourage you to build the habit of reframing your mindset, your conversations with others, and your perspective on the goings-on of the every day.

Chapter 4.
Use Your Voice

DO YOU GUYS like The Little Mermaid? Do you remember it? Because I used to fucking love The Little Mermaid. I loved Ariel so much that I would wrap my legs up in a towel so that I would have a fin. Then I would find the closest thing that resembled a rock. Then I'd borrow my mom's bra, and I'd sit on my rock (it was a chair) with my fin made out of a rolled-up afghan blanket. Flapping my fin, I'd sing the songs from the movie. I didn't want to be like other Disney princesses. Just Ariel. Until Aladdin came out on VHS, that is.

One of my least favorite parts of the movie is when Ariel gets her voice taken away. Now, granted, Ariel—well, the bitch had it coming to her. She literally traded her voice away in exchange for a chance at love. Now, I love my current boyfriend very much, but I don't know if I would want a lifetime of laryngitis for him. I digress.

Anyway, it was the worst part because you're watching this young, headstrong, strong-willed, and stubborn woman who only wanted love and was punished by having her voice removed. She couldn't say how she truly felt or what she wanted.

As a little girl, I pitied Ariel. I could not imagine not being able to use my voice and speak my mind. Yet, here I am, in my twenties, still healing from those who stifled my voice and muffled it through emotional and verbal abuse. How did I, so easily and quickly, allow them to take something so important from me? My power. My opinion. My voice.

When I was nine years old, I used to sit in my family's living room and watch Oprah interview these women who had found their voices after having gone through situations like rape or abuse. These women had lost their voices due to being traumatized, feeling alone, or becoming utterly helpless. I remember Oprah, time and again, sitting across from her interviewees and turning to the audience and the camera urging us to, "Use your voice and speak up." I remember not understanding. Now, as a woman, who wears the scars of someone who allowed others to silence her for years – I get it now.

When we don't use our voices, we are not emboldening ourselves. We are not speaking our minds. We internalize whatever it is we're feeling or thinking—the raw emotions of anger, depression, and sadness that come from being violated in some form. We swallow these things, and as a result, our body absorbs them. I truly believe that they develop into manifested physical illnesses and ailments.

We, as women, are finally able to step up and use our voices. It has not been easy. It has not been the norm. As this book goes to press, the #MeToo campaign is trending all over social media. It speaks to women finally stepping up and using their voices and speaking about their courageous stories of being victimized. It's taken a while to get there, but we are well on our way.

Unfortunately, even in 2018, using our voices is not the most popular option. This is not to say that men don't struggle to speak up about what they need or how they feel, but this book is written for the kickass women in my life and all over the world, so I'm writing this for you.

Once you start using your voice more, it'll get easier to do. I remember when I started my methods of healing, people would look at me cross-eyed when I would use my voice and speak up if I was hurt or offended and in turn, set some boundaries.

"Uh, are you okay?"

"Who are you?"

"What happened to the old Hope Alcocer?"

I remember the first time I spoke up to my now ex-boyfriend. He looked at me and said, "I don't remember you being this assertive." Was it unattractive? Aggressive? Surprising? I didn't think so. Did it come off that way? Maybe. Why? Because it was foreign to him.

There came the point when I decided that I would always use my voice, even if it is the unpopular opinion. I will warn you, it will not be accepted at first. Sometimes even your family will be taken aback and may even give you the cold shoulder, but in time, as they see that this is the new you, they will come back and accept you with wide open arms. Using your voice within your friend group can sometimes be harder than using it with your family, because, let's face it, at the end of the day, your family has to love you. I mean, isn't that what family's about—unconditional, never-ending love?

Your friends, however, are not required to do anything. They choose to stay in your life. But even though you don't want to step on toes, you shouldn't do something that makes you uncomfortable. Say no. Why do something that makes you uncomfortable?

Let's talk about being uncomfortable. I know there are quotes all over the Internet right now, memes plastered with the background of Mount Everest or some really vivid lake and stream with trees somewhere in Washington, that tell you to go beyond your comfort zone. But there's a difference between being uncomfortable and being anxious. The more you learn about yourself, the more you will grow. And once you do that, you will achieve self-actualization. You will be able to figure out where your boundaries lie.

Even harder than using your voice with your friends is what you dread the most—using it at work. If people don't like what you say when you use your voice, you can very well be fired. That's your meal ticket. That's your rent payment. That's your Whole Foods grocery bill. That's your DryBar blowout. But you know what? If you don't use your voice at work, you will not be respected, have an identity, or be able to succeed.

Speak up at the right time for both yourself and your boss. I mean, come on, you're an adult. Learn the art of timing. Think first, and then act. I don't need to tell you this, right? This isn't a Carte blanche to throw up your middle fingers and say "FTW" to every Tom, Dick, and Harry. Speak up when you feel like you're incorrectly criticized. Speak up when you want to see changes and you feel like it will better yourself, your community, your workplace, your family, your friend circle, and your life.

Use your voice in your relationships. It is one of the hardest things to start out a relationship not using your voice, for fear that he or she may leave you, only to turn around and start using your voice when the relationship is on the rocks. Your boyfriend or girlfriend will probably look at you and say, "What the hell has gotten into you?" You'll have to explain that you've been swallowing your beliefs, your values, your core, your personality, and your identity because you didn't want him or her to leave. Start now. Start while this relationship is new. Start when you want to say something. If they're right for you, they'll welcome your input.

One more thing: don't turn into a "yes" woman. If your plate is full, use that voice of yours and turn them down. This bleeds into self-care, of which we will talk about later on in this book.

Practice using your voice. It's like a muscle. Be like Ariel. Push yourself up on that rock, on your fin made of an afghan blanket, and use your voice.

Chapter 5.
You Don't Have to Swallow

YOU DON'T HAVE to swallow. I'm sure that if you glanced at the chapter list for this book, you thought that this one might be a little bit disgusting. I'm sure that my mom is less than thrilled that this chapter made it into the final product, but I knew that this one needed to be talked about. When I say that you don't have to swallow, I'm sure that the entire male population reading this book, or perhaps the boyfriend of anyone reading this, really wants to get upset with me. However, just hear what I have to say. Disclaimer: if you're easily grossed out, or conservative and don't like the word moist…move on.

I love giving head and receiving oral sex. I love foreplay. There is nothing that makes me hornier than watching my partner get turned on. There's nothing sexier than that. If I could choose between receiving pleasure myself and giving my partner pleasure, I would always choose the latter. My favorite thing to do is swallow. Because when I swallow, it means that I have satisfied my partner.

But you don't have to swallow. Again, you're probably thinking: What the hell? What is she talking about? Do I spit? Contrary to the chapter title, this has nothing to do with that. It's about expectations. Society decided that it was a requirement to pleasure your partner in whatever way he chooses. I use swallowing as an example, but it can be anything sexual that makes you uncomfortable and isn't something that you want to do. For me, it's something that I love to do, but that doesn't mean that everyone else wants to do it. And that's okay.

I've lost track of all of the times that one of my friends has said that she's gone on a date—a first date, no less— and when she starts making out with the dude, things escalate. There's some touching on the upper half, and before you know it, her head is being pushed down there towards his sweaty ball sack. I pause her there and say, "I'm sorry. They do what? Your head was pushed where?"

"Oh, yeah. He pushed my head down toward his crotch."

"Why?" I once innocently asked. This was the first time I heard this.

"Well, because he wanted me to give him head."

"Did he even ask you if you wanted to go that far? Did he ask you if that's something you'd be into on the first date?"

"Well, no."

"Well, then why would he push your head down?"

She shrugs. "Because it was assumed."

That, my friends, is the problem. It was decided that the man will dictate how far it goes physically. At some point, it was decided that we as women are to feel guilty if we don't do things like swallow or if we don't make him cum first or if we don't like a certain position.

Who, in what world, decided that a man should orgasm first? Where is the logic in that? Sex is about pleasure. It's about intimacy. It's about serving someone else so that the other person you care about or are intimate with is pleasured. Who in God's name decided that the man gets to go first? You know normally I guess I wouldn't care if the dude came first sometimes, but it's the fact that once they do climax, they're not in the mood or horny anymore. They just roll over or talk about how they want buffalo wings. Like, helllllllo, I'm not done yet. What are we women left with? Feeling unsatisfied, resentful, now dry as hell. We are always left unable to have an orgasm.

I should notate here that there are guys who just think their partner is so goddamn sexy and can't take it anymore, so they do cum first, only to make sure their woman is pleasured equally if not more. And I'd like to take a moment and a sip of my almond milk latte to thank them for being the unicorns here. I find, though, that a man who is not cognizant of the need to be self-less in the bedroom seems to have that lack of character carry over to other aspects of their life. If they're selfless in bed, it's safe to say they're selfish IRL.

Speaking of IRL, who decided that we have to put out on the first date or we're undesirable? Who decided that if we don't swallow, then it's not sexy? Who decided that we even have to give head? Who decided that we need to take it in the butt? Who decided that we need to do it doggy-style? Who decided that we need to call him "Daddy"? Who created these standards? I don't fucking know, but you don't have to uphold them. Sex is about intimacy.

This is not to say that you can't have a one-night stand. I mean, I personally can't get rubbed off, wet, and ready to go for a one-night stand. For those of you who can do it and those of you who enjoy it, by all means, go get it. Have a one-night stand. For those of you who crave intimacy and love, you, unfortunately, are in a world where it is expected that a man's sexual needs will overpower yours. This just goes back to using your voice and making sure you're in a consensual situation. Otherwise, this will lead us to feel dirty, used, unsatisfied, and lacking self-esteem. You decide where it starts. You decide what it entails. Break the expectation that you need to put out first and that he needs to finish first. Those are unrealistic, unfounded, and illogical standards put in place by some chauvinistic, selfish man who didn't get the memo that women are equal to men and that we are to be treated with respect.

The next time that you're on a date, I ask you to consult with the inner you and ask her, "Is this even something that I even want to do?" If the answer is no, then step back. You should never be made to feel that way. Your sexual experience should be just as pleasurable and enjoyable for you as your partner.

I urge you to reconsider and speculate on the situation the next time that it happens. (Hopefully, it won't.) Girl, you don't have to swallow, but if you want to swallow, then have a hell of a time doing it. You'd better walk away just as satisfied as the lucky man who nailed you in the first place.

Chapter 6.
You Only Need Three Things to Live (and it's Not Him)

I IMAGINE THAT YOU'VE glanced through the chapters of this book, and you're probably thinking: Damn, she must have been through some shit.

Take it from someone whose loved one has walked away. You can learn this from your friends, family, career, or relationships. Humans are meant to be loved and to seek companionship. We are not meant to be alone. Some people can't handle being alone. Harsh reality—no one ever died from that. If you are alone in life, you can still succeed. The people surrounding you do not define you.

Yeah, the title of this chapter sounds harsh, but I say it with a good intention. The point of this chapter is to tell you that you can want to be in love. That's fine. But you don't have to. It's okay to be by yourself! Healthy, even. Truthfully, we only need three things to stay alive as human beings. We need air, water, and food. Everything else is secondary. You don't need love or companionship. I know you're going to try and argue with me on this one. Scientifically, my love, you do not need love to live. Everything else is optional. Everything else is icing on the cake.

The word need is a strong word. By telling someone that you need them, you are giving them something more than your love. You are giving them power over you. As women, we have already relinquished enough of our power to men by force. To give it to them willingly is to essentially give up your identity. If you need them, then what are you without them?

As babies, we use our power to cry for things that we actually need to develop. When we become adolescents, we start using our power to make decisions about where we will end up in life and how we will get there. As women, we must channel that power into acting graceful, tough, unbending, and yet willing to compromise where it is needed.

Instead of saying that you need someone, tell him or her that you care for them and value their opinion. Without them, life still carries on. To the person who's just gone through a terrible breakup and feels like a hollow version of herself, I say to you that you'll be fine. You will. I promise.

Chapter 7.
Not Everybody Is a
Photographer (The it Factor)

WHEN THE DIGITAL camera suddenly didn't cost as much as a Midwest mortgage, it was like everyone in my age bracket was suddenly a photographer. Then before I knew it, when social media blew up, everybody needed a profile picture, right? Everyone then learned how to edit their photos so that they could look their best on the Internet. This led to filters—more accurately said, about eighteen million filters slapped onto one picture. Then, before you knew it, you call yourself a self-made photographer and make a Facebook fan page for your "photography business." Then you do some family sessions that include your own family sitting on the same goddamn bench or random ass couch in a field for each picture. And, voila, you're a photographer. Right? Wrong.

After that rant, you probably think that I'm targeting photographers. Let's use my industry as an example, so you don't think I'm hating on a stay at home mom with a point-and-shoot camera. Being in the digital media sector, and everyone thinks that because they know how to post a tweet or schedule something that they know what social media management means. Frustrates me to no end! Just because you see a couple skills about a topic, does not make you an expert.

See, this is not just about photographers. I've just been using that example since I got invited to two dozen Facebook fan pages for friends' photography in 2012. It's about the distaste and my annoyance with the lack of professionalism for those who do something a couple times and decide they're an expert in it. I'm also able to reflect on this after spending much time in both the music and fashion industries. The people I now work with are different than a decade prior. This induction into a different level of talent has lent itself to the frustration of true photographers, or professionals in any industry feel when someone just walks by and slaps on the label these people have worked so hard to obtain. True professionals have actually developed their skill sets, educated themselves about their equipment, and are not some self-proclaimed expert whose experience includes a session of a kid in a basket in the corner of their living room taken with an iPhone every now and then.

Rant over.

Once you have taken the time to date your equipment and obtained the skills needed it to make it your industry of interest, you need to figure out what will separate you from the rest.

What's your IT factor?

My what?

Your IT factor. What is separating you from everyone else in your industry, your genre, your sector? Find that, harness that, and utilize it to obtain your success.

There are a million photographers.

There are thousands of social media strategists.

There are a million and one musicians.

What is going to set you apart? What will make you stand out in your oversaturated job market? Everyone has the it factor. You just have to find it. One of my favorite things to do, in my free time, is help loved ones hone in on their it factor. It's like discovering a new brightly colored wardrobe in a closet they didn't know they had.

If you had an internship at a really cool place, you're not automatically a big shot. Just because you have a set of skills, it does not make you marketable. Just because you have experience, does not make you better than everyone else. No, you need the "it" factor.

It doesn't matter what industry you find yourself in—if you don't have the IT factor, you'll get swallowed up whole. People tend to focus on where they went to college and what degree they have or their certifications or where they've interned. At the end of the day, none of that matters. You must have it. Think about what makes you different. You're interviewing for a job against two hundred people. What would make the recruiter select you?

You need to take a couple of things into consideration. Your appearance is the first. No, not how skinny you are. DID YOU NOT READ CHAPTER TWO? I do not mean if you look like you just came out of a plastic surgeon's office. I mean, how do you present yourself? Are you polished; are you poised? Do you look the part? Do you stand out?

You need to be able to converse with human beings in real life. Our generation doesn't know how to have personality. We don't know how to have pizzazz. We don't know how to have poise and people skills. People tell me that they love my bubbly nature and the fact that I can hold a conversation. That's part of my it factor.

The third thing is your level of energy. I believe in the law of attraction. If you're in a room of two hundred people at a networking mixer, what is the vibe you are putting out? Fuck off? Or are you smiling, are your arms uncrossed and off your waist, do you look approachable?

If you are reticent, then you won't attract the conversation that you need.

Jot down ten things that set you apart. What is your it factor?

Chapter 8:
If He Says He's Not Like Every Other Guy, Then He Is Exactly Like Every Other Guy

WE ALL WANT it. We all want that one guy who's not like anyone else. We all want that one guy who proves that he's different from everyone else. We want that one guy who totally breaks our expectations. We want the guy to sweep us off our feet and be our knight in shining armor. We want someone to prove to us that guys are not all the same. How do you find him?

Well, you don't find him. He'll find you. But, in the meantime, there's one line that they all love to say when you begin to vocalize your opinion that all guys are the same. "Oh, I'm not like every other guy," he'll say, all suave, as he tilts back his glass.

Naturally, you'll bring up the fact that you're skeptical, and you'll mention how many times you've been burned. Maybe you'll bring up an actual situation about a friend. In turn, he'll list all of the reasons that he's not like every other guy. Maybe you'll exchange numbers. Maybe you'll text each other, and you'll start to let your guard down. You'll say, "Hmmm. Maybe he was right when he said he's not like every other guy." And then you'll let your guard down some more. Maybe you'll go out for a drink, two drinks, a date, two dates, and then you'll start to notice his douchebag tendencies. Oh, but wait. He said he's not like every other guy.

Any guy that has to say he's not like the others are covering something up. A guy who's truly not like every other guy will show it through his actions. He will show it in how he texts you. He will understand boundaries, meaning his level of communication will healthily lie between blowing up your phone constantly and texting a dead rock. He will offer to pick up the tab even if you're a strong, capable woman. Does he ride the L home with you, or pay for your Uber home? Does he make sexual advances when you've said that you're not feeling it tonight? These are all telltale signs. Little hints, little flags, good or bad, that we love to ignore. A guy who has to constantly speak to his character and integrity most likely does not have either one. A guy who actually has them will demonstrate. His actions will be his resume.

I have learned this the hard way. I have fallen for the guy who thinks that it's a game to conquer women. He spoke about his character all the time. But he was a jackass. He was just trying to get into my pants.

Before I head into my thirties, I just want to take a trip down memory lane. You don't mind, do you?

Looks Good on Paper Guy

Maybe he'll take you out for a really great meal, show you a fantastic night on the town. Your mama fucking loves him. "Oh, why can't you just be with so-and-so?" she'll ask. "He's perfect for you. He's so respectful. Blah, blah, blah." That's just the surface. It's like a resume, which is perfect on paper, but when put to the task, maybe you find out that he fibbed a little here and there. We tend to be so desperate to lock it up that we ignore these signs. I urge you to get to know him before you jump in deep. Put him through a sort of job interview. He can wine and dine you as much as he wants, but he probably doesn't have his shit together.

This type of guy—the financial analyst, the restaurant owner, the hotel manager, the private investigator— they're so suave and debonair, and they kiss up to your friends. But I'm willing to bet that they're up to something. Are they emotionally available? Do they respect your boundaries? Do they let you take the lead when it comes to intimacy?

Just Doesn't Take the Hint Guy (aka the ex)

Next up is the "just-doesn't-take-the-hint" guy. In my case, this was my ex. You have ignored him. You have removed him from social media. Maybe he's your ex-boyfriend, and you have broken up with him once, twice, three times…okay, let's be honest, eighteen times over the span of the last ten years. There's that guy who just does not get the hint. They will reach out to you on holidays as if nothing's happened and no time has gone by. They will pop into your Instagram DMs and reply to a story as if you guys have been carrying on a conversation the whole day.

This type of guy does not get the hint, but the real issue here is that he doesn't respect you. He didn't respect you when you broke up with him. He didn't respect you when you politely declined his invitation to dinner. He didn't respect you when you removed him from Facebook or said you could no longer see him. My best remedy is to block him. As harsh as this sounds, act like he does not exist. Remove him from your life. Make it impossible for him to get in touch with you. Because as long as he is able to get in touch with you and have a foot in the door, he feels like there is a chance.

It took me nearly fifteen years to get rid of my guy. I wish I had done it fourteen years sooner. By blocking every chance that he has to connect with me, I've been able to move forward and be happy. It's like this type of guy has some sort of radar. The moment that we're happy and moving forward, he'll try to dash back in. Block him. When you have a wart, what do you do? Freeze it off.

The Wannabe Bullshitter

The wannabe bullshitter can take the form of several different types of people. He can be the starving artist, the wannabe musician, or just someone who garners sympathy because he tries so hard and is so sweet. He's the one who will do an Instagram video of himself strumming on his acoustic guitar, making girls swoon and then be a total douche bag in real life. He's the one who will be super sweet and sensitive to status updates and tweets. When you connect with him over lunch, you will think that he actually gets what you're saying, because he's this sensitive guy. However, you notice he's able to do this with every girl he meets. So, does he really just understand you, or is he just a master of saying what you want to hear?

But he doesn't do anything with his life. He just sort of exists. I've encountered a couple of these in my life, especially in the music industry. And while they may, in fact, be charismatic and talented, they're most likely the guy whom in high school had the acoustic guitar at a bonfire serenading five girls at a time. He probably had a puka shell necklace on too. And you thought that was it. You thought you had found your future husband. He's sweet. He looks great with plugs and his five o'clock shadow. Oh, he got a new tattoo. And you connect, right? Because you're connecting with this emotional bad boy who has some sort of dream that he just can't achieve, you start to open up. You start to let your guard down and think, Oh, maybe I could help him. Maybe I can save him.

Usually, these wannabe bullshitters are yearning to be saved. But guess what? You're not the only one saving them. No, if this type of wannabe rock star, poet, artist, or writer hasn't gotten it together and is coming to you to be fixed, chances are you're not the only one trying to fix him. Unfortunately, when I was trying to save this one guy, so were four other girls.

Be leery of a guy without direction. Be leery of a guy without any potential. There's nothing worse than falling into a trap where you think that you're the person who's going to save this guy who's living in his parents' basement, only to find out that he really had no intention of doing anything with you other than fucking in the first place.

The Pen Pal

This type of guy is the most fucking complex. You meet through a dating app or on Facebook, or maybe he slides into your DMs. Maybe you'll meet at a bar, and you'll exchange numbers. You'll text. You'll text a lot. You'll text all day. And your phone is chirping all throughout work, and you get distracted because he just sent you a lot of kissy emojis. He blows up your Snapchat. But then it comes down to a really big, life-changing question: "When are we going to meet?" you'll ask. "We should meet up," you'll hint. And somehow he'll dodge it. He'll "LOL" at you.

This, my friends, is the guy I call the pen pal. He likely has nine other text conversations open. He's only contacting you to boost his ego, to distract himself from his boring life. I mean, who wouldn't feel good about themselves with their phone constantly vibrating and chirping? It makes you feel good, right? I mean, let's be honest, anytime you've talked with someone via text or gotten to know someone, and they are complimenting you and patting your ego, you feel pretty good. Right? I mean, who wouldn't? Hey, you're allowed to. You're human.

But someone who's not willing to invest more than 160 characters into you really isn't worth your time. If you sense that you've gotten involved with someone like this, call him out right away and say, "Hey, do you have an intention of meeting me or going out to dinner?" Call him out on it. Give him one opportunity to be frank and upfront, and if he says, "Haha, IDK. I'm really busy." then move the fuck on.

The Ghost

The fifth type of guy I've run into is "the ghost." This one used to really upset me.

You meet at an event, and he's your perfect millennial hippy with a slight hint of a lumberjack. You'll exchange numbers. You'll start talking. Everything's going well. You talk sun up to sun down; or maybe he's more of a chilled, laid-back guy who likes to have healthy gaps between his conversations. Or maybe it'll actually escalate to a first date or a second date.

Everything's going well, and you're thinking, Oh, my god. I actually found a normal one. And then the texts get fewer and less frequent. He goes from texting novels to you to one-word answers. He'll respond to the conversation eventually, but then his reply makes no sense like he wasn't even a part of the conversation. You'll start to wonder, Is this thing on? He's ghosted you. You think it's going well. You think you're doing great. You think you're quite a catch. There's chemistry. And then, one day, out of nowhere, he just ghosts you.

I know this sounds like cliché, but you should realize that the problem isn't you, it's him. Congratulations! We live in a society where many people don't think we owe anyone a damn thing. That's right, because nowadays, if we don't like someone, we can just POOF, disappear! It's beyond me why this is okay. The equivalent to this a thousand years ago would have been for me to be in mid-sentence talking to a man, and for him to turn around and walk away.

That's not acceptable. That's not okay. But we live in a world where people feel that they're allowed to hide behind a screen, that they don't owe anyone a damn thing. Many people don't have any decency anymore. They're cowards. Instead of saying that we no longer see eye-to-eye, they'll just stop talking.

If you are ghosted in your dating life, do not reach out. Do not beg for anyone's attention, affection, validation, love, or affirmation. Do not do it. Do not constantly text to see what they're up to. Trust me, if they're interested, they'll contact you. They'll contact you consistently. Okay? The only ghost we like, the only friendly ghost, is Casper.

Every guy that I've listed here has started out with "I'm not like every other guy." If they were truly walking what they were talking, they wouldn't need to say it. Stop settling for any of these types of guys and just work on yourself in the meantime. Love yourself, date yourself, work on yourself, and please take heed if a guy says a phrase like this. You'll be better off for it, trust me.

Chapter 9.
Getting Married Is Not
the Be-All-End-All

GETTING MARRIED IS not the be-all-end-all. I realize that this chapter may not be the most popular, especially with my audience back in the Midwest. To that, I say—I love you, and I'm happy for you. Things that I've written in the past have both been written with a true and full heart, while others with a broken one. And as I write this chapter, I can honestly say that my heart is fulfilled, as I have recently found love. I'm not writing this chapter with a jaded heart. I'm not writing this chapter looking through the lens after two broken engagements. Since I was five years old, I've been trying to race to the altar. And for the longest time, I thought that getting married was the be-all-end-all. Think about it. Our society trains us that that is what we are to do from the moment that we're little. Every Disney movie ends with the princess getting married. Countless Barbie dolls are donned in wedding dresses. Weddings are celebrated everywhere, in every single movie, all across the world. It just seems natural that if you don't get married and that's not the end goal, then you have your priorities wrong.

I bought into this, especially coming from a religious family. My mom had always trained us that while she wanted us to have careers and goals, we were also supposed to get married, move out, and make babies. While her viewpoint has changed in the last decade, especially after seeing fallout after fallout, heartbreak after heartbreak, that is how we were raised. So you can understand why I was dead-set on finding a husband.

I had dreams of going to college, making something of myself, and being successful, but in my mind, no matter what I did or how I succeeded, I wouldn't be someone until I changed my last name and had a sparkling ring on my left hand.

Those beliefs and that skewed viewpoint were heavy influencers on the chapters to follow. I immediately got into a serious relationship during my senior year of high school. I carried that relationship all throughout college. While he was not the best fit for me in any way—we were two different personalities from two different worlds—I was set on making this one work because I wanted a husband and I wanted to be married by my early twenties.

When the relationship became too stressful, I dropped it. Don't be fooled. I did not walk down the steps of independence to single womanhood. Cue the Beyoncé "Single Ladies" dance. No. I immediately jumped into the arms of my best male friend. He and I both shared the dream of being married because, we, just like everybody else in this world, wanted to be loved. We wanted the white, picket fence life. We wanted children. We wanted the promise of commitment and forever. That one didn't work, either. Shocker.

I, however, bounced back quickly and fell into the arms of my second ex-fiancé, who kindly brought to light many things that I needed to work on personally. But we didn't work together. He left me several weeks before the wedding. Did I hate him? Absolutely. Was I livid? Definitely. Was I hurt? Yes. Was I mortified? You betcha. Did I eat cupcakes almost every single day and gain an additional forty pounds for about a year after the breakup? Hell, yeah.

I was so depressed because I thought I had found my person. There was no more looking. There was no more dating. There was no more swiping right or left on an app. There was nothing. I had found the person with whom I wanted to spend the rest of my life, or so I thought. I was willing to wear whatever pair of rose glasses to look at the person whom I was dating and see him in the light that made him my future spouse. But the universe had other plans.

Here we are, five years later. While I am in a wonderful and satisfying relationship, but it has taken me years to realize that marriage is not the be-all-end-all. I am working on the art of living in the moment and enjoying living in the present, as nothing in life is definite. Because for the last couple of years, I have been okay with being alone. I've been working on myself quite a bit and battling a lot of issues that have stemmed from these fallen and broken relationships. But I have found myself, time after time, taking myself out of the situation and saying, "This is what happiness looks like. I am happy. My heart is happy. I feel good, and hey, I'm not married. I am at the top of my career right now. Things have never been better. I am successful. Money is not an issue. I'm able to look around and say, "Hey. You did this, and you're kicking ass in New York City, the greatest city in the world."

Guess what? I don't have a wedding ring on my hand. I don't have a husband waiting for me back home. I was able to achieve true happiness without changing my last name and having a marriage certificate. Is it something I still want? Absolutely. I will be so happy when it does happen if it does happen. Do I plan on getting it? Hell, yeah. Do I know when? No. Will it be the end of the world it I don't get married? Nope, I'm pretty sure worse things can happen.

When you learn to love yourself, you don't need another person to remind you of your worth. You don't need marriage to be the finish line or the end game. It would be nice, sure, but it's not the vein of your existence.

There are other ways to achieve happiness, and to be yourself, and to find yourself.

Marriage is an individual decision. There's no time table. There's no right or wrong. There's no type of wedding you need to have. Also, marriage looks different for everyone. You can sleep in two different bedrooms and still have a-rockin' sex love. You can have five kids. You can have no kids. You can live in separate parts of the country, and commute back and forth.

Society tells us that perfect life and complete happiness is having the same last name and a new set of tax exemptions. We must have a white, picket fence; three or four kids; a non-shedding dog; and a living room that looks like it was made straight out of Pinterest. I don't think that's true. I don't think that's the be-all-end-all. To my friends who have found this and deem that as their happily ever after and their be-all-end-all, I congratulate you and I'm happy for you, just as I am happy for the women and men in my life who do not have partners.

I think it's different for everyone. I think at some point we need to accept, and not judge, and just realize that everyone's walk is different, and there is no standard. We cannot hold ourselves to someone else's standard. We should not determine our own happiness based off of someone else's.

Now, do I still have Pinterest boards for my future wedding? Absolutely. Do I have a ring picked out? Shh. Don't tell him. Do I have a couple of dates set? I mean,

I can dream, right? But in the meantime, I'm still happy. I'm still fulfilled. I'm still living a beautiful life. Marriage isn't the endgame, and I realize it's not the end game for everyone around me, so take it slow. Take a deep breath. Own your life. Love your life. Make it the best life possible, and love and marriage may follow.

Chapter 10.
Your Parents Did the
Best They Could

I WENT TO SCHOOL for psychology, and in a nutshell, they tell you that parents are responsible for everything. It seems to always go back to childhood and early development. Most things. I understand that and respect that to a certain extent, but every single class that I took had these underlying themes throughout my degree program. Your upbringing and those who raised you were the core of who you would one day become.

These theories probably started with Sigmund Freud, of who I don't know if I can really believe considering he had a lot of messed up theories about his mother. I remember a quote my punk ass would always post when I was an immature twit: "We are the ones our parents warned us about." or "Those who criticize our generation forget who raised it." We have become very comfortable with blaming our parents for everything and not taking responsibility for our actions. While I believe that is true to a certain extent, as far as our development and growth are concerned, our parents did the best they could, and it took me thirty years to realize that because every therapist that I saw told me that it all stems from my parents. Freud probably has something right, although I'm grossed out by his theory that the son always wants to fuck his mom.

Sure, psychology might be right, but my heart tells me that my parents did the best that they could. Some of your parents probably had it rougher than you think, and we, as their children, often have no idea. Instead of throwing up your middle finger at them and disrespecting the values that they taught you, tell them that you have a new way of doing things. Even when you didn't want to go home because you weren't sure how bad things would get after you did something wrong, you still realized that your parents probably did everything out of love. I understand there are some bad apple parents too, but I won't try to speak to that. What I will say, is that even if you have a terrible relationship with them, try to put yourselves in their shoes. Consider their background and their upbringing. Was life hard for them? Were they abused? Did they have a trauma happen in their life? I would also be willing to bet that if they had any sort of trauma, it's unresolved and not worked through. That'll impact a person, trust me. They likely did better than their parents did, and you will do better than they did. Aim to consistently improve the cycle, as I'm sure our children will do better than us too.

As you come to terms with the fact that they did the best they could, perhaps the healing can begin. Maybe you'll have to make the first move towards healing or changing patterns – take it in strides. Apologize, where you think you may need to, and hopefully, they will apologize, as well. Make amends. And if you have a positive standing with your parents, then keep nurturing that. They did the best that they could.

Chapter 11.
Abuse is Abuse

WE LIVE IN a time when, finally, people are able to come forward and feel safe to admit that they're struggling. Something I'm noticing is that close friends of mine are coming forward and saying, "I was abused," "This happened to me," "I was harassed," "I was molested," "I was raped." But, as they have come forward, other girls who have been abused, perhaps not physically, are still hiding in the shadows. He didn't hit me, but he slapped me, so it's not the same thing. Oh, he never hit me, but he would scream at me constantly.

Abuse is abuse, and it counts for anything that makes you feel violated and uncomfortable. Everyone has a different threshold, too. Abuse is abuse. It's a violated boundary, and it needs to be recognized. It can be physical, mental, or emotional. It cannot be held to the standard of others around you, either. Everyone has their story and how it impacted them. Sadly, abuse is quite often done by the people we love and trust. It is your trauma. It is your scar. It is your story. Whether it be with your family speaking to you, your first boyfriend going too far, someone at the club being too handsy, or your fiancé pushing you into a closet, it's abuse.

There's never an excuse for abuse. There may be an explanation, but, fuck, there's even an explanation for why someone murders someone. There is never an excuse. There's never a situation in which abuse is okay.

Thankfully, enough women are finally vocalizing their pain and suffering and are speaking up. As I'm writing this, my Twitter feed is blowing up because people are coming forward and saying #metoo. We are in a time when our voices are no longer silenced, and we're starting to realize how far our voices can carry.

It's so important to realize, though, that while some voices may carry louder, and be a part of this movement for all to say, some voices may be quieter and not wish to share their story—this is okay. Everyone's voice sounds different. In real life, you may have a friend who has a higher-pitched voice than yours, a lower voice than yours, or a more nasal voice than yours. They're all still voices. And they matter. Everyone speaks about their abuse differently – some may not wish to speak about it at all. It's okay.

We each have a different story. Each person's situation is different from the next, but it doesn't make it any less valid. Abuse is abuse. There are some things you can do to get help. Without sounding like a 1-800 hotline, here are some low-key ways to start to heal your pain. Talk to a girlfriend who has been through it, too. There can be healing in camaraderie. Begin to process this yourself. Journal. Download a meditation app. Cry. Dance. Yell at a chair and pretend it's the abuser. Healing begins the moment that you start working on it. Own your story, hug yourself, and take the first step to work through this, whatever that means for you.

Chapter 12.
Stop Saying Yes

HOW MANY TIMES do your friends text or call and say, "Hey, what are you doing right now?" My first inclination is to stop and think: Wait a minute. Why are they asking what I'm doing? Do they have a plan? Do they have something to which I'm going to have to say yes or no? Oh my God, I totally can't say no. I have to say yes. "Yes," I answer in my head. They haven't even asked the question yet.

We are so used to saying yes out of obligation to everything and anything. Whether it be a baby shower or an event or buying someone the leggings with the bizarre prints on them. We have mastered the art of saying "Yes, I'd love to!" when we really don't want to. It's a lie. We have mastered the art of the lie.

We've somehow mismatched respect and kindness for lack of respect for ourselves and just trying to please others. Where does this leave us? Tired, grumpy, depleted. Behind on our work and hobbies. Unfulfilled, and before you know it, we've said yes to everything, and we're now double-booking and trying to find time just to get in a session at the gym or make a home-cooked meal.

Somewhere along the lines when quote graphics off Pinterest told us to step outside of our comfort zones, we've mistakenly thought that meant that we shouldn't have a comfort zone. You don't need to say yes to everything. There is a balance between stepping outside your comfort zone and tossing away boundaries and schedule to appease everyone else.

If your first initial gut instinct is to say no, it's probably the answer you should go with. You should want to go out with your friends. You should want to go out on the town. You should want to go out on a trip with your girls. But if you feel that tug and say to yourself, "I really don't want to go," then it's not for you.

As we eliminate the things to which we say yes when we really want to say no, or how about a rain check, we will find ourselves being more and more fulfilled and having more energy to actually do things instead of always being depleted.

Being an author and micro influencer means that I'm invited to a lot of events. If I had eighty-six hours in the day, I could go to all of them. But sometimes I'm just too tired, and nine times out of ten, I don't even want to go, but I don't want to say that right off the bat. For some reason, that's rude.

You don't want to say yes, then cancel, and look like a flake. Something I've learned is to just pause and say, "Let me check my schedule. I don't have it in front of me, so I'll get back to you." Or, if you actually have your planner in hand, say, "Let me check on a couple of things, and I will get back to you."

Give yourself some time to breathe and recalibrate once you're out of the anxiety of that situation. Ask yourself: Do I really want to go to this event? Will it make me a better person? Would it make me a better *insert your career profession here*? Are there people there who can help me with my career? Will I feel tired or fulfilled?

If you go to an event that deals with your career, you will likely be inspired. But if you're going to your friend's, cousin's, sister's twice-removed bridal shower and it doesn't behoove you at all, it doesn't serve you. Not that everything has to serve you, but if it's not going to benefit your relationship with someone or better yourself, say no. Learn the art of no.

I would imagine that is a great skill to use when you become a mother if you're not already a mother, or when you're a wife, particularly when you have familial obligations and other people aren't pulling their weight. I've watched the women in my big Armenian family never, ever say no and in turn, they're worn out and overworked. I think learning the art of saying no and pausing before you say yes is a beautiful concept we lost sight of because we were too busy nodding our heads instead of thinking about what we want out of our lives and what it'll take to get us there.

Chapter 13.
College Isn't for Everyone

OH, THIS ONE is really going to make mothers love me.

Is this punk girl telling us that college isn't for our kid, which is encouraging him or her not to get an education? To be a dropout? Listen, that's not what this is about at all. If you haven't figured out that not all of the titles are what they appear to be, then maybe you need to re-read again.

Storytime. When I was 17, I was prepping to graduate high school early. I ended up having a head injury due to being given the wrong medication, which resulted in a grand mal seizure. I hit a tile floor and plenty of other hard objects, which resulted in some memory loss and cognitive difficulties later on. It included six months of rehab and nearly a decade to follow of natural and alternative rehabilitation methods because I had some hormonal and psychological imbalances.

I tell you this story, while you may have heard before, to paint the picture and let you know that the start of my college education was not typical. However, now looking back, it has allowed me to see college and the experience it holds for many different people through a different lens.

My parents had insisted from the time I was little that I was to go to a four-year school. There was no other option in our household. They were even willing to help pay for it, which I know is something most kids' parents don't necessarily have to do. I was blessed enough to be receiving additional financial assistance as well.

So one would think that college was going to be the way to go. It would be easy, it would be simple, it would be relatively cheap, and I would be able to come out on top with a career in which I could do well. When my brain injury happened in 2005, and I just wanted to take a year off—maybe go back, maybe not. My parents were insistent on me going to school. In hindsight, I'm glad they pushed me to go through some sort of educational program. However, five and a half years of school later and nearly $75,000 in student loans, I wish, and they (my parents) do, too, that things could have been done differently.

College is extremely hard. I say this in general, for anyone without the difficulties I had but also because of my particular situation. College was so fucking hard. I had short-term deficits and had to have extra time to take tests. I had severe anxiety when it came to taking tests. Most professors didn't understand where I was coming from. If I weren't using flashcards, bright colors, recall games—and taking three times what it normally would take a typical college student to study—I would fail the class.

My first year at community college, I did great. Easy peasy, right? The second year of school, my sophomore year, I attended a private university from which I was academically dismissed for poor grades due to this entire brain condition. This further placed a bad taste in my mouth for school. What happened to grace, understanding and supporting your students? That's another topic for another day.

It wasn't until I got into public university that I was able to finish my schooling. I got involved with a great learning disability team that helped me the best they could. I was able to choose from several professors who were fine with me creatively regurgitating information just through essays, presentations, and things of that nature. And there were more resources and support available for someone like me in my situation.

Again, this is just my story. I know it is not your story, and I know it may not apply to you and your college journey or maybe to that of someone you will know in the future. However, I tell you this story to let you know that hindsight has caused me to realize that college may not be for everyone. For me, it was due to medical circumstance. For others, it may be the fact that it just may not be for them. Maybe they can't afford it. College isn't for everyone. And somewhere along the line, society deemed that unless you go for another four years after high school, you won't match up with other people—or think you won't match up to other people.

This does not mean that you should not be educated. Ah-hah. There's a difference. I believe that people think education equals college and that's not necessarily true. Learning a new skill and educating yourself beyond your field of study should happen even if you have a degree as well. Your journey to seek knowledge and self-actualization should not end when you accept your diploma. There are plenty of ways to learn, regardless of whether you're 18 or 80. Let me do another disclaimer here. I do believe there are some jobs for which college is necessary. If you think I want a brain surgeon working on me who only got their Associate of Arts, you're out of your fucking mind. A surgeon needs school. A lawyer needs school (though I think I'd make a fantastic lawyer, what with all of my valid and indisputable arguments with my boyfriend).

College isn't necessarily the route all people need to go to succeed. And if they choose not to follow it, or if they choose to explore it and don't like it, I do not believe that they should be held to a different standard or looked at through a different lens just because one person's path is not the same as "the norm".

I'm not here to tell you to drop out of school tomorrow and go tell your academic counselors to fuck themselves. If you like college, stay there. If it works for you, stay there. If you need college for your future career, then keep up the great work. But don't condescend to people who don't have a degree. There's still such an attitude surrounding those who have decided college isn't for them.

We waste our lives by worrying about what our own lives look like through other people's lenses. We live our lives by watching other people's movie reels unravel on social media, 24/7, 365 days of the year. In turn, it allows us to create this notion in our heads that we need to follow someone else's path and journey to be as happy as they are. This is not the truth.

You don't need to follow someone else's plan to a T. If this were true, if we were supposed to follow the same blueprint of life, the "American Dream," it would mean that we all would marry a certain type of person and be in the same line of work. All job markets would be oversaturated. It would mean that we would all choose to look the same and have the same style. It would mean there wouldn't be Republican/Democrat parties. It would mean that there wouldn't be countless religions because we would all have the same belief system.

If we are encouraged to be different in every other aspect of our lives—sexually, spiritually, aesthetically, and so on—why should educational paths be any different? College isn't for everyone, and someone's blueprint for his or her life is not for you. You need to define your own set of goals. If that's college, great. If that's just graduating and continuing on with extra classes, great. If that's going to get your Master's and three PhDs, good for fucking you. But don't live your life measuring with someone else's ruler.

Find out what you want and obtain it in a way that is right for you.

Whatever you do, though, don't ever stop learning. So even if a college degree isn't for you, I do encourage you to always learn. Pick up a new book. Grab an audiobook. Try a class. Get a certification. Because the flipside to this is that if you choose not to go to college and not to pursue the four-year, get yourself ready to compete against people who are trained and educated professionals. I'm not saying that it's right, but it's the way the world works. Counteract that with experience and your personal it factor (Chapter 7, y'all).

Plenty of successful people did what they're doing without college degrees. The most successful people in the world did not go with the status quo. Because one's plan, one's journey, does not make it your quest. If that were true, the path we walk would be overcrowded. We'd be carbon copies of each other.

Chapter 14.
Mental Health Is a Thing

MENTAL HEALTH IS a thing. I have a friend who has witnessed me go through anxiety and mental health struggles for more than a decade. She's been sympathetic at times. But then, when we're discussing other people's mental problems, or she's watching other people's struggles on social media, or she's viewing different charity organizations speaking about cognitive issues, she'll tell me that mental health is not a thing.

I look at her—this beautiful, successful woman who gets the runs every time she goes to work and wonder how she cannot relate to me. I see a confidant who is so afraid to make a professional move that she's remained in her hometown for nearly a decade. My heart goes out to someone who makes up every sort of health excuse every time that she's submerged in a crowd of people—and I say, "How can you not understand that mental health is a thing?"

Mental health is, indeed, a thing. As a matter of fact, one in four people in this world, according to the World Health Organization, will be affected by mental or neurological disorders at some point in their lives, and around 450 million people are currently suffering from such conditions. Mental health disorders are among the leading causes of ill health and disability worldwide. That isn't a statistic made up by BuzzFeed or Elite Daily. This is a real thing. Mental health is a thing. Mental illnesses are a thing. Now, my personal take on mental illness is that I'm not a fan of labeling someone with a textbook disorder and loading them with drugs so that they can't feel for the long term unless it is extremely serious. Again, my personal opinion. I am an advocate of working through trauma or issues with the help of a support system and a trained professional. If that includes medication, so be it. Everybody needs something different.

I do believe in the reality of mental disorders, and I do believe in support. I believe in healing. I believe you can get better.

Whether it's something as small as just not liking crowds and feeling some generalized anxiety or something tremendous like living with bipolar or multiple-personality disorder. Mental health is a thing. Maintaining your mental health is a thing. It's so important. Unfortunately, as usual, social media has turned this mental illness thing into a huge, trending issue that people can openly and anonymously hate on. We have someone like my friend, who will look me in the eye and tell me, "It's not a thing," as she's scratching her stress hives or running to the bathroom to take a poo because she's in a "crowd" of more than five people. Then, at the other end of the spectrum, we have people on social media who are claiming to be "triggered" whenever they get upset. As someone who struggles with PTSD, anxiety, and depression, I find myself revolted by these clueless millennials using this term that is used for people with actual mental health issues.

As usual, our society doesn't know the balance on handling an issue, but whatever happened to just understanding that mental health is a thing and that there is plenty that we can do about it? The first thing that you can do if you feel like your mental health is off is to find out what's wrong. Seems simple, right? It can be a process, trust me. I do not mean self-diagnosis. I do not mean hopping onto WebMD and answering their three hundred questions or clicking all over the model that is supposed to look like you to figure out what you have.

Again, we overuse the words within mental health far too easily. "Oh, this TV season ending is giving me depression," or "I'm triggered because Kylie Jenner's pregnant." That's disrespectful, so don't do that. These are real things we deal with, and I actually loathe when people on social media utilize those words to signify superficial emotions. It would be like someone with a paper cut saying, "I have leukemia." You don't do that. You just absolutely do not do that.

Mental health, I would venture to say, is maybe even more important than dealing with your physical health. It's important that you treat it sensitively and that you understand what's going on. The worst thing that you can do is self-diagnose. You will never get it right. I promise you that. I'm not saying that you have to spend a fortune on a psychiatrist with eighteen different degrees on his or her wall, but I am challenging you to go to a professional—whether that's a wellness practitioner, a psychologist, a psychiatrist, or a counselor. Take the time to go figure out what is actually going on. If you think that your insurance won't cover the cost, then go to my website (psst, look on the back of the book). You will see resources that have helped me out before.

Once you figure out what's going on, figure out how to get better. There are so many different routes that you can go. We are so blessed that we live in a world where alternative therapies and wellness treatments are available. Of course, your typical means of getting well would be to go to a therapist. I have found my therapist through the Talkspace app, but I'm blessed that she lives near me so I can go to her office when needed.

Through the app, I am able to send her as many video messages or voice memos that are needed to convey my point or issue. I'll send screenshots of friends or family members who are upsetting me. I ask, "How do I handle this? What do I do?" and she will help me through it as though she is right there. My selected monthly membership allows me to do this five to six days a week with my therapist. Sometimes I only need her once a week, but her help has been absolutely incredible. My point here is to get yourself some sort of means of mental health care.

I know that they can be expensive. Fortunately, there are many wellness clinics, especially in the bigger cities, that cater to the millennial who may not be able to afford help. Your insurance company will definitely have mental health practitioners who can guide you every step of the way to determine what works for you.

One tip that I have is that you need to date your therapist. I mean that, because I've been through three different therapists, and it took me to see this one who truly understood my personality and how to speak to me when I needed a come-to-Jesus talk. It is so important to find someone who truly understands you. Go for a couple of sessions, and if you still don't feel like you have that connection, then that person is not the right therapist for you.

This does not mean that you need to feel on top of the world when you see your therapist every single time. Many times, the problem gets worse before it gets better when you're in therapy or doing any kind of treatment.

I can almost guarantee this. You will not feel better instantly, but it's a step in the right direction.

Many people ask me where I stand on mental health and medications since I talk so openly about it on social media and during interviews. Because of my past history with health issues, I'm not the sort to reach for prescriptions. I don't usually advocate for that, and I honestly don't know much about it, so I'm not going to sit here and write another thousand words on the different medications you should try. What I do know is that medication is not for everybody, but it works for many people. Medications have saved lives. Some of the people in my life I am closest to use medications to help with depression, anxiety, bipolar disorder, multiple-personality disorder, and suicidal tendencies.

But please, love, just don't let yourself become numb forever. When we suppress our emotions, flashbacks, and triggers with medication, we very well may find that five, ten, or fifteen years later, something will revive itself and rock our world—in the worst way possible.

Then there are those who have found a combination of different therapies. We have dance therapy. We have play therapy. We have acting therapy. We have acupuncture. We have diffuse oils. We have group therapy. We have yoga. Find a combination of what works, and make it work for you. Investigate what's out there and which form of treatment best resonates with you.

Consider a healthy combination of several different mental health treatments. Everyone is different so it may take a couple different things for you to feel better and see an improvement. Go to yoga on Sundays, see your therapist on Tuesday. Get a prescription for Xanax. Whatever works for you. Realize that you are unique— there's no one in this world just like you.

Chapter 15.
A Leopard Doesn't
Change It's Spots

WHEN I WAS little, my mom often used car rides to teach us lessons or have awkward AF conversations. I mean, think about it, it was brilliant. We couldn't go anywhere until we arrived at our destination. Us kids quickly caught on, though, and asked our mom questions that were just as awkward or thought-provoking.

My mom never spoke an ill word about anyone. She never wanted to worry us kids with adult concerns. But one day, a particular person in our life struck a chord. I now know why, but at the time, I didn't understand why my mom had this distaste for someone when she was never like this with anyone else.

She told me, in very elementary terms, what this person did to her and her family.

I asked, "Well, how do you know they can't change?"

"Because, most times, more often than not, a leopard doesn't change his spots."

I, at the time, didn't realize what this meant. She explained it to me, but my mind was still running rampant with thoughts of National Geographic specials on PBS with spotted felines chilling in trees.

What she meant was that people do not change. They modify and adjust, but it is hard to change. Unless proven otherwise, assume that what you see is what you get. And while there are exceptions to every rule, it would serve you well to remember this simple rule. You weren't locked in the car given nuggets of wisdom your whole childhood by my mother, so I'm just catching you up to speed.

I'm not saying there aren't exceptions. I'm not saying that most people don't make complete life overhauls. We modify, we adjust, but it is hard to truly change down to our core.

I would even venture far enough to say that even if we do "change" and it's a "brand new us," that when faced with adversity, it could potentially result in pushing the metaphorical reset button back to the default version of ourselves.

I have found this to be extremely important with ex-boyfriends. And I have, unfortunately, found this out the hard way when I have welcomed an ex back into my life for the second, third, or fourth time. I did this for over a decade.

This time will be different. He'll change.

But then, I was royally disappointed when he falls short and acts like the same self-absorbed prick that I left the first time. What did I expect? Why did I expect something different?

If someone is going to change, it won't happen in a matter of months. Or weeks. It will take a substantial amount of time. Time will be your best friend as you wait and see if a person has truly changed or just made some adjustments to temporarily satisfy the situation. In my experience, that kind of change is rare. So don't count on it, don't hold your breath. You will never regret waiting to make sure someone is moving in the direction of true change. You will, however, regret getting burned by assuming they rid themselves of their spots.

Guard your heart, loves.

Chapter 16.
Find a Mentor

S O, I'M GOING to burst your bubble and share some wisdom that my mother bestowed upon me when I was a little girl. "Hope," she would say, "you do the best you can. You try your hardest. You don't just give it 100%. You give it 200%. You don't just do what's expected of you. You go the extra mile. But, Hope, no matter what, there will always be someone better than you. There will always be someone that is not as skilled as you, but there will always be someone to aspire to be, to idolize, to want to be, to strive to be. There will always be someone better than you."

I remember hearing that and thinking, "Wow, so I'm not going to get the Disney Channel mom that tells me that I'm the best ever, and has an entire wall of my accomplishments, and writes a Christmas letter with two pages specifically dedicated to all I've done." I just wasn't going to have that mother.

And looking back, I'm actually glad that I didn't have that kind of mom, because that type of mentality, to hear that someone will always be better than you, keeps you from stagnating. It doesn't allow you to be okay with where you are. It has caused me to strive to be even better.

But something that has allowed me to continually strive to be better, something that has continually allowed me to seek more success, is having a mentor. Now, I have had a couple of different mentors. I currently have a few different mentors. They may not even know that they're my mentors, in some situations, but I have various people in my life who I put on that pedestal for a particular thing and who I hold accountable.

I have a mentor who is in publicity which helps me with my efforts in that area. I have a female entrepreneur mentor, someone who I actually do work for on a contractual basis. I admire her and ask her questions about how she has gotten to be where she is, and she has turned into my mentor.

Lastly, I also have a godmother, who also just happens to be my aunt. She is one that throughout my entire life I have been able to look to for a new perspective. She also helps me see things through someone else's lens. She has taught me empathy and acceptance just by her own actions. She is also one of the few people in my life who can tell it like it really is without her head being bitten off by yours truly.

So, you have your professional mentor, you have a lifestyle mentor, and then you have a personal mentor, and those mentors can be men or women. They could just be people that you look up to or want to trade places with. But don't be quick to knock your own life. Ask yourself, "How did they get there?" Chances are, they have their own mentors. Chances are, their mentors have mentors.

Now, a mentor does not necessarily mean that you would want to Freaky Friday it, but that you can point to different facets of that person and say, "Yes, that's what I want to be. That's who I want to be." You can even have a mentor from afar, someone who doesn't know he or she is your mentor, but you just observe and emulate them.

You can also have a conscious mentor, when you say to someone, "Hey, I admire you. I admire X, Y, Z about you. I was wondering if you have any time, can you give me guidance in those particular areas?"

But if that person can't mentor you, do a little research. Did he or she write a book? Will he or she be presenting at a conference that you can attend? Did he or she have a mentor who can help you attain what you wanted in the first place?

A mentor does not mean that you are a copycat. And I say this because there are several women in my life that express an interest in being me to my face. Actually, they flat out said, "I want your life. I wish to be you," and they copied me to the very T. I mean, the way their Instagram handles are structured, the way they tweet, the color scheme they use, the verbiage they use, you know? That is mere imitation, and that's not really a mentorship because a mentorship involves an attribute, a career path, a lifestyle that you wish to emulate. Do not steal someone's brand—just work hard to pave your path to look similar, but not identical.

Do your part in the mentorship. If this is a conscious mentorship, or even if it's not, even if you just say, "Hey, I admire you. You're an amazing boss. I'm a manager at my company, but hey, you're the director, and I admire you." Do your part to let that person know that you appreciate him or her because it does wonders for people in leadership positions to hear that they're doing a good job and their efforts are being noticed.

The best means of creating and inflicting change on the world and in our society, especially as women, is to lead by example,

so when someone notices that we're doing something incredible or something noteworthy, it just means a lot to be told about it, so let people know. Send them a thank you note. Send them a postcard. Put something in their mailbox, or on their desk, and just say, "Hey, the way you handled that the other day, I admired it. I aspire to be you. Thank you. Thank you for being an amazing person. Thank you for being an amazing woman. Thank you for being a great leader." Let them know.

Check in when you can. Let them know of your successes; and if they're holding you accountable for failures or challenges, let them know the high points, too, so that you're not just going to them with the negatives or when you need something. Say thank you regularly. You don't have to necessarily give a gift. Just say thank you. Let your mentors know that you are very grateful for their partnership.

And also know that sometimes you outgrow your mentors. The mentors I had five years ago, the people I admired five years ago, are not necessarily the people I respect today. As you hit each milestone, if you're following your path correctly and healthily, chances are you're either equal to or have surpassed the mentor you once aspired to be five or ten years ago. Sometimes you outgrow these people. Just say thank you and move forward.

Most importantly, be a mentor yourself. Pay it forward. Give back. Chances are, no matter where you are in your life, there is someone who looks up to you, and I invite you to take the time to turn around and look over your shoulder. Who is watching you? Who is looking to be guided by you? Who is reaching out and asking questions? Who is complimenting you? Who is aspiring to be you? And see how you can help them. Ask if you can guide them. Ask what you can do.

Hey, in this society, this culture, we women will not grow if we don't help one another. So, as you find a mentor, I invite you to be a mentor, as well. This is a beautiful synergy that I like to call the art of the successful woman.

Chapter 17.
Nobody Cares

OH MY GOD, what a bitch. How could she say something so harsh? I care! Slow your roll. Before you start assuming what this chapter is about, I'm just going to give you some honest insight as someone who has dealt with social media, social presence, online presence, digital presence, blah, blah, blah over the last eight years.

I would not have a job if we didn't have social media. While I love it, it has really turned our world upside down, because everyone knows everything about our lives all the time. There are actual clinical diagnoses revolving around social media. There are things like social media and Facebook depression.

I use the Talkspace app, as I mentioned before. We actually have a support group for social media stress. It's for people who feel down and alone and inadequate because they see everyone else doing things on their feed. When I see that I'm like, "How could social media be such a good thing if this is what it does to people?" It's absolutely mind-blowing.

The point of this chapter is just to urge you, whether you do social media for a living or whether it's just something you enjoy as a hobby, to remember that nobody cares. I mean that, even for myself.

Part of my job essentially requires me to discuss and showcase my work, my accomplishments, and my projects. But at the end of the day, very few people genuinely care about what I do with my time. No one gives a fucking shit what I do with my life. No one cares how many copies of my book that I've sold. People don't care if I've found love again. People don't care that I've been engaged twice.

Back in the days before social media, people didn't brag about their accomplishments. The most you would get, even ten years ago, was a student-of-the-month award or a spot in the local paper, and that was it. We boast and brag about our accomplishments all the time on social media. At the end of the day, nobody cares.

Back in the old days, did everyone know what you were making in the slow cooker that night? No, they didn't. They absolutely didn't. They didn't have Facebook to tell everyone what is for dinner or if your kid had a successful shit on the little kid potty or not. If we're going back to the pioneer days, they would maybe talk about it when they were riding side-by-side in their covered wagons along the Oregon Trail. They'd be like, "I skinned this chicken, and then I added this to it, and it tasted great." That was the extent of bragging.

Sure, some people do give a shit. But, odds are, those people already know about your accomplishments. If you put everything out there, you'll turn most people away.

Again, I completely acknowledge in my own profession, and similar professions, there are certain accomplishments and career achievements that require us to put our lives out there, but we have to balance it out. Hell, sometimes I do want my ego stroked. I'm still working on this. I do know that we have to balance it out because people just don't care.

I saw this quote a while ago: "Work in silence. May your success be your noise." I thought to myself, How beautiful is that? Even for my own book, I remained silent until I published it. I didn't update anyone on anything. It was so explosive because people were like, "What the fuck, I didn't know the book was actually coming out."

I love that mantra: work in silence. Don't let everyone know all of your projects and what you're working on. It's obnoxious as fuck to update the world on a daily basis what you're up to. Nobody ever died from not airing out their dirty laundry to everyone who will pretend to listen.

Chapter 18.
Be Selfish

WHEN WE THINK of the word "selfish," we envision something negative. I get that. It makes perfect sense. When I was little, my mom would tell me to share a toy with my sister or to be nice to my brother or to keep it down a little bit while she took a nap. She would say, "Hope, don't be selfish." We have, of course, associated the word "selfish" with negativity. While that is typically what the word means, I'm here to tell you that it's okay to be selfish sometimes.

As you know, I am in therapy on a regular basis. It's something that I plan to do for as long as possible, whether it's a monthly maintenance check-in or for an emergency. Our bodies are like cars. Our minds are like cars. Our hearts and souls are like cars. If we don't do regular maintenance, everything will break down at once, and then we'll be without a vehicle. We'll be running, but we won't be able to do much. If you're walking away each day drained and not feeling like you are fulfilled in any way, that's when, in my opinion, it's time to be a little selfish.

Now, a lot of people call it "self-care," which we will talk about in the next chapter. I've referenced self-care so many times in this book. It's about time we talked about it, right? Today, it's just okay to go with the mindset of being selfish. My therapist, when I tell her about issues that are going on at home or work, will say, "Well, what does Hope want?" I just look at her like she's speaking French.

Unless it's illegal, immoral or puts your integrity into question, it's okay to do what you feel you need to do. It's okay to be selfish sometimes. That means that if you don't want to go to that event tonight and you already paid for your ticket, and you promised your friend, you can still back out. You don't owe anyone an explanation as to why you can't go. You can just say, "You know what? I'm sorry. I just can't make it." That's it. It's okay to be selfish. It's okay to take a seat on the train, unless, of course, there's someone who needs it more.

I come from an Armenian Orthodox family, and my grandma is still working in the church with every fiber of her skin hurting because she is so worn out. She doesn't even take a moment for herself because she doesn't want to be selfish. This is a woman who, over many holidays, will be ill. She'll have vertigo, but she'll still produce a seven-course meal. She doesn't say anything. She just suffers quietly because she doesn't want to be selfish.

We always tell her things like, "Grandma, you don't have to do that. You don't have to. Grandma, ask for help. We can go eat at a restaurant. Let's get you checked by a doctor. Grandma, retire from all this work you do at the church" but she doesn't do it because she doesn't want to be selfish. Her heart is so huge. She loves so hard. I just wish she would love herself a little bit too.

My mom is the same way. She's selfless. She lost her first husband when I was six weeks old. He died of leukemia. He died, and she had to take care of a six-week-old baby (me) while mourning the love of her life. She didn't get to be selfish. I don't think she knows how to be.

I remember, when I was three or four, she was working full-time. She took us to Disney World. My mom had the flu, and she still took us to Disney World because she didn't want to let me down. She didn't want us to wait because she didn't want me hurt or sad or upset or lacking something. I remember my mom putting me in the bathtub at the end of the day, and she was just not able to move out of bed because she was so sick. I remember asking her what was wrong. She said, "I just don't feel very well, honey," and acted like it was nothing. The woman pushed through the flu with her toddler at Disney world. This is just an example of the countless times my mom put us first.

She also put her career on hold to raise three children. She put off her day-to-day activities to homeschool three children. She had her life on hold every weekend to take care of me after my brain injury when I was in college. She picks up each one of us every time we stumble or fall, every time we have a downward spiral, or a twist, or a turn, and every time we get hit with a curveball. She will change her schedule. She will cancel everything. She refuses to be selfish.

Now, that's noble. It's beautiful. It's admirable. Yes, you're right. You should be selfless. You should think of others. Most of the time, that's great, but sometimes you need to deny others and embrace yourself because when we deny ourselves what we want, we become resentful. It may not happen all at once. It may not happen that day. Or that week. But at some point, we will feel resentful.

When we deny ourselves self-love in any form, we become, at some point, resentful toward the world. It can be one person. It can be a group of people. It can be immediately. It can be delayed. But we will become resentful. When we become resentful, we treat others poorly. We lash out. We hold grudges. We have anger. We show symptoms of that anger. We become imbalanced. We isolate ourselves and withdraw from others. Then we stop giving 100% in our relationships.

It's a vicious cycle. If you don't give a little, you'll become resentful. If you're resentful, you stop giving. It's important to be selfish sometimes, so you have the energy to be selfless when it matters.

Chapter 19.
Adopt Self-Care

THE WORD "SELF-CARE" has been used so much in the last two years. My therapist uses it all the time with me.

Okay, new drinking game: every time I say the phrase "my therapist," we take a shot.

Just kidding, but as I write this book, I'm forced to recognize how much I bring up my experiences in therapy. May this show what a positive, earth-shattering impact that me taking care of myself and my mental health has been for me.

Anyway, my therapist (ayyyy, take a shot) takes self-care days two times per week. On Wednesdays and Sundays, my arm could be falling off, and I could have had three mental breakdowns, and my therapist will just not be available.

When she first told me about self-care, I was like, "Huh, okay. Another hit-me phrase," but when she explained what self-care was, I was intrigued. I thought to myself, I can't think of anyone in my life that takes self-care days. Most of us don't have the luxury to say, "Peace out, boss. I'll see you later. I'm going to take a self-care day," but self-care is simply taking time for yourself. I told you that it's okay to be a little selfish. That just means choosing what you want once in a while.

Self-care doesn't mean giving the finger to everyone around you. When I started self-care, I'd say to my boyfriend, "Fuck you. Don't talk to me. Don't ask me for anything. No, I can't do this thing. It's self-care. Don't talk to me on self-care day." I would just go MIA.

You don't have to be a bitch when having a self-care day. You don't have to be bougie about it, either. When I began practicing self-care, I immediately started spending money, because I somehow equated that with self-care. You can do those things if you have the funds and that is what makes you happy. It's all about what fills you up. Most of us, however, cannot afford to do that level of socialite self-care on a regular basis.

Here's a list of things that you can do to take care of yourself, just to get you started:

1. *Go on Groupon and buy yourself a monthly facial or massage.*
2. *Walk through a bookstore.*

3. *Sit near a body of water.*
4. *Check your community calendar and look for free yoga or a free fitness class.*
5. *Doodle in coloring book.*
6. *Get the weekly manicure deal at your local nail salon.*
7. *Diffuse a calming oil. Hate lavender? I do too. Try a citrus or peppermint oil.*
8. *Journal or record a voice memo on your phone if you hate writing.*
9. *Watch a YouTube video of reflexology and practice techniques on yourself.*
10. *Volunteer for a cause that makes you get emotional and cry. That will be the one you put your heart into.*
11. *Work out for at least 20 minutes.*
12. *Learn a new skill.*
13. *Take a free course on a site like Coursera or Udemy.*
14. *Buy a cheap bottle of wine and sit at home in your underwear.*
15. *Pick five colors of pencils, pens, crayons and draw random shit.*
16. *Clean your room.*
17. *Get a hair or bang trim.*
18. *Cook a new recipe.*
19. *Call your mom (or someone who inspires you).*
20. *Sit in front of your mirror naked and find three physical attributes you think are hot.*

21. *Watch a Disney movie.*
22. *Make a dream (or inspiration) board.*
23. *Put on your headphones and discover a new artist through Pandora, Spotify, or Apple radio.*
24. *Light a candle and just sit still.*
25. *Work on diaphragmatic breathing.*
26. *Put your phone in airplane mode.*
27. *Install the Anti-Social or Freedom app.*
28. *Delete apps from your phone that stress you the fuck out.*
29. *Clean out your inbox.*
30. *Masturbate. Yeah, I said it.*

I encourage you to figure out what works for you. Then, be consistent. Take care of yourself as much as possible, and once you do that, you can take care of others. Be selfish, and then be selfless.

Chapter 20.
Set Boundaries

WHEN I FIRST started seeing my therapist one of the first Jesus talks we had, so to speak, was to set boundaries. I told her my whole life, how I grew up, my family dynamic, and everything. She said, "The first thing we need to do is set some boundaries." Now, when I thought about boundaries, I also thought about bubbles. Specifically, the stranger-danger bubbles that I believed in when I was little. Quite honestly, that's exactly how boundaries work. It's saying, "You're in my bubble." I realized that I needed to set boundaries even with my loved ones. They felt the need to comment every time that I changed or didn't want to hang out when I came home.

Boundaries. It's the magic word. It's the magic word that no one in this society can understand. We think it means to be selfish. We believe it's only for people who have mental health issues, but it's a word that needs to be used around the clock and also applies to many different people in various situations. It can be putting your phone on "do not disturb." It can be telling your mom, "Mom, I love you, but that statement was hurtful." It's when your boyfriend is trying to move things along, and you say, "I love you. I want to be with you, but I'm not ready to move in together yet." It's not answering your clients at 2:00 am with their Skype messages or calls.

It's telling your boss, "No. Actually, I can't stay late for the fifth night this week," or "Hey, can I tackle that next weekend?" It's telling your best friend when she's been an absolute bitch. It's telling the charity that you volunteer for that you need to take a break. These are awkward, painful, difficult things to say. They're uncomfortable. They're weird. They feel foreign. I promise. It gets easier. I promise that once you start setting boundaries, you'll love how good it feels. You'll want to set more boundaries.

I blame technology for the "be on 24/7" mentality. Think about it. We are always readily available and reachable at any given point in time. We are a text message, a phone call, a tweet, a DM away. People know that we're always on our phones. This, in turn, has people assuming we're available at everyone's beck and call. Facebook, Instagram, Messenger—they all tell other people the last moment we were on our phones by showing when we were last active.

Setting boundaries can be hardest with our families and those closest to us. As I'm writing this book, my phone is currently blowing up with notifications from my friends and family. That's fine. I can text them all day long, but I don't need to reply right away.

When you set boundaries, speak up without sounding accusatory. Remember that you can convey what you need to say and those limits you need to set without being a cold-hearted bitch. If you go berserk while claiming your boundaries, people will pull away. Remember, don't be drastic. Baby steps, baby steps.

Be honest and say that you're figuring out your expectations of yourself and of others. Usually, once you set boundaries and explain it for the first time, people will think you're a badass and admire the hell out of you. Tell yourself it's okay to set boundaries. Tell yourself that you're always a good person. Tell yourself that you're still loved, and you can still love others. At first, you may even feel like you're doing wrong. You'll be consumed with guilt the first several times. This is almost a guarantee. Just try it. Practice this new mentality.

Sit back and watch people respect you. You, in turn, won't feel so depleted.

Chapter 21.
Collaborate, Don't Compete

I'M SO IMPRESSED that over the last year, more and more women are coming together and using their gifts to make great things happen. This is so important, and I feel like it needs to be enforced even more. I feel like we've just gotten started.

I remember several years ago when I got involved in the music industry; it was so hard to find another woman who was willing to share her experiences with me. It was every woman for herself. And now, as we head into a volatile era where we need to collaborate, we are collaborating. I'm relieved about that. Women are coming together and saying, "Me, too. I've been there. I understand what you've been through." Now that the floodgates are open let's keep them that way.

Just a few years ago, the ladies over at Bumble developed the ability to give its user a BFF through the phone.

On the one hand, this is so sad that it even has to come to that where we have to use an app with an algorithm that's designed to help us find friends. It's sad that we have to turn to technology and use a dating app to find someone to be kind to us. On the other hand, what a beautiful thing that a company so powerful and socially conscious created a platform for that.

We like to keep to ourselves as women. When we discover success or tricks that can be used to enhance ourselves, we like to keep them to ourselves for fear of someone using them better. But what if we let go of our pride and allowed others to have a hand in success?

All too often, we compete. I want you to think about it. When you walk into a room, and there are other women around, what do you do? I'll be completely honest with you. Many times after I dart for the food table, I'll look for other women. And because we are naturally insecure, we size them up. We scan the room for contenders and have our guard up.

I have to work on this all the time! Especially when my self-esteem is lower than usual that day. I'll think to myself; She has a smaller waist than I do. Or, I would kill for her boobs. Man, I think to myself, her butt looks great; much better than mine. I'll obsess over their conversation if I can hear them talking about their career. Is this behavior embarrassing? Yes, it is. But do I do it? You bet. We size up women. We see what they're wearing, how their hair is cut, whether their complexion is good or if they're a little bloated. We size ourselves up. Again, I'm not saying it's right, but we do it. But it's really sad because we're all the same. We're all beautifully different at the same time.

Women are beautiful. They're beautiful inside. They're beautiful outside. Their souls are lit on fire with passion and yearning to make the world a better place. I think that if we looked at women more as sisters and as friends, knowing the element of love and community we have in womanhood, in sisterhood, no matter where we are in the world or where we are in our walk of life, then we should accept one another.

We should feel safe around women, safe collaborating with them, safe sharing hopes and dreams. We should not feel so alone. I believe that if we all adopted this mindset, the power, and the love would exponentially increase.

We need women to survive. We need women to move forward. We all do. And I cannot imagine what would happen if we adopted this notion that we should collaborate and not compete. Over the last year, and during the turn of events following my first book, I have reached out more and more to women with a mentality of, "Hey, you have this skill that I don't have. Your strength is my weakness, and perhaps my weakness is your strength. How can we collaborate? How can we get together? How can we work with one another to just exponentially increase that power and clout?"

For the men reading this book, this mentality can apply to anyone. You men seem to work among yourselves. But seriously, I'm shocked at how little collaboration men need. You guys do this weird "island unto yourselves" thing. Hell, I wouldn't be surprised if you just grunted to communicate, like cavemen. What would happen if you pushed yourselves beyond your comfort zone? What would happen if we didn't hoard our success, momentum, and dreams, but opened up to other people?

However, don't always trust people with your ideas. Be open, but be cautious. As a freelancer, an independent contractor, and an entrepreneur, I've had to build a level of trust and understanding before I tell people about my ideas for the next five years.

Put yourself out there, but with a cautious tread. Step outside of your comfort zone and just look to build each other up. Support the women in your life instead of supporting some stranger. This does not mean I want fifty additional Facebook invites to join your leggings group, but if you know a friend who makes quality goods that you need, buy from them instead of a stranger. Support one another and build a level of community and collaboration instead of jumping to compete. Ladies, together we can rule the world. Excuse me; I'm going to listen to some Beyoncé.

Chapter 22.
Make Time to See Your Grandparents

THERE WAS A children's book, which I used to have my mom and my grandma read to me when I was younger. It was called The Giving Tree. It was by Shel Silverstein. Maybe you kids of the 90s are familiar with some of his books. Most of them were illustrations, with words to go along with them. He was famous for The Giving Tree, which told the story of a little boy who had a tree. As children, who didn't have a tree? We all had a tree growing up unless you guys were city slickers. Maybe you climbed up a concrete building or something.

We all had a tree that we would climb, would maybe put our initials in, would use as our fort, would hide behind. We would have it be our little space. We'd climb it and pick apples. This book told the story of this boy who had a tree, and this tree was more than just a tree to him. He turned to it, like I just said, for his shelter, for his food, for his playtime. His imagination ran wild with this tree. The tree fed him by giving him apples. Apparently, it's a cute little-animated tree. The tree represented a figure in the child's life that is a life source, and it displays unconditional love. For some of us who have hard, demanding lives, maybe the person who represented unconditional love, like a parent or a grandparent, is gone. If that's the case, my heart goes out to you in these pages because I'm speaking about unconditional love, and maybe your person is gone. For that, my heart goes out to you.

Regardless if they're on earth or not, I'm sure you can relate if you've ever had someone who has gotten you from Point A to Point B. Your true north, your life preserver. They've never left your side or forsaken you. I've been so blessed in the life I've been given. While I've had so many hardships from a very young age, I've been very blessed to have my parents, my aunts, and my grandparents be that source of unconditional love. Going back to the whole story of The Giving Tree, the tree represented that source of unconditional love.

The story is about this boy who grows up. He's a little kid, and then he becomes a little prepubescent kid who probably is starting to get some hair in places he didn't know hair was supposed to be. Then the book shows him being a teenager, a young man, and then a man. All throughout this time, all throughout this progression, this growth, this boy is turning to his tree for resources. He's turning to it for food, shelter, a place to sit, or shade. He wants to climb the branches. He wants to sleep in the tree.

The story takes a sad turn because the boy starts to use this tree. He begins to take advantage of the tree. The book shows the boy when he has become a man. He goes back to the tree, and he's like, "I have no money." The tree gives his trunk, and he goes, "Make a boat." I'm paraphrasing here. You guys should read the book. If you're parents, get the book for your kid. If you're not parents, get the book for one day if you ever have kids unless you don't have kids, because as we talked about earlier, getting married isn't the be all and end all.

Anyway, as I was saying the young man goes to the tree and says "I have no money." This tree gives his fucking trunk, and he's like, "Make a boat out of it. Make a house of it." The tree says, "Make something cool with it." The boy comes back, now an older man. He's a fucking leech, this dude. The tree goes, "I'm sorry. I have nothing left to give you. I have a stump. I have my very last breath. I have my stump." It shows the illustration of this older gentleman sitting on this tree stump. I think that's how the story ends. If you have any heart when you read this book, you're going to cry like a baby. You feel so bad for this tree. For the love of God, there was no save the trees movement or something back then!?

This book reminds me of those in our lives who give, give, give, give, give. I realize some of us may not have had someone like that in our lives, but I'm willing to bet that at some point in your life you had someone showing their unconditional love who would give the shirt off their back. The tree reminds me of a grandparent in many respects. My heart always thinks of my grandma when I think of this story because my grandma gives, and gives, and gives, and gives. A lesson I've learned over the years is it's so easy for me to get lost in the shuffle of hustle, bustle, busy, crazy city life. When I start dating someone, I get wrapped up in that. I forget to call Grandma. I forget to call Grandpa. I forget to call my parents. I think it will suffice to text my mom, be like "hey, love you." It doesn't do as much as if I was to give her a call, be like, "Mom, how was your day? How are you? What's going on in your life? Forget about my life that you see on social media, as well as 10,000 other people, but how are you doing?"

I think this is especially true with the older people in our life. I can talk all day about how I've let family down and keeping up communication, but I want to speak especially today to the elders of your life, whether it's grandparents or a great-aunt, or a great-uncle, maybe an elder in your church, perhaps an old boss who is retired now, or maybe someone you used to visit when you volunteered, and you visited them all the time at a nursing home, and you've let it lie. We get busy. When we get busy, we often get selfish. Yes, I know Chapter 18 told you it's okay to be a little selfish. It's always important to give back to the older adults in your life. Make time and call your grandparents. Again, if you don't have grandparents in your life, my heart goes out to you, but I'm willing to bet that there's someone older than you, someone wiser, someone smarter, someone who loved you when you needed to be loved, and that perhaps you let that relationship fall to the wayside.

My grandparents, to the backstory, helped my mom during a very trying time in our life when I was younger. I remember in my head so vividly every Sunday we were at their house with all the groups of the family together. These were the gatherings that my grandparents lived for and always looked forward to. They would have the table set on a Wednesday when we went on a Sunday. After my immediate family and I moved to Michigan, those visits became fewer and fewer, and further in between. Then eventually it would be every other month. Then eventually we would only see my grandparents a couple of times a year. For a while, I would never call my grandparents. I would never keep in touch with them. I was horrible at it.

When I think about it too long, I want to cry because my grandparents were like the Giving Tree. They gave, and gave, and gave to their daughter, to their grandchildren, to their son-in-law, to their nephews-in-law, to their nieces. Then things fell by the wayside. We got busy, and there were social media, and distance and our lives made us forget about the glory days when our grandparents stopped their lives and captured the moments with us. I always think of this. Over the last two years, I've had to work on it because it's so hard to make an excuse for being busy. Over the last two years, I've been trying to spend more time with my grandparents. I go back and visit. I sit there, and I talk about their lives.

I hear story after story. Sometimes they may be repeated, but I sit there, and I listen. I savor every moment. I stop, and I pause. I live the moment with them because I know at any point they could be the stump of a tree and say, I have nothing left to give. They can be in their last years, in their last days. I'm going to wish I didn't take, take, take, and I gave, gave, gave. Again, this doesn't apply to just grandparents. It applies to your parents, your big sister, your great uncle, your teacher, your professor, anyone in your life who's older and wiser, smarter and has been influential, and you took, took, took. Don't just use people and leave. Give back to them.

When you have a heightened point in your life, don't just stay in touch then, and when it dwindles have the relationship fall by the wayside. Honor the Giving Tree in your life and give back to them in the way which you think it will be best received and the best way that they will know they're loved unconditionally, just as they unconditionally loved you.

Chapter 23.
Stay Current

I HAVE HAD THE blessing, privilege, and honor over the last couple years to do cool interviews, and I'm honestly not anybody special. I promise. Like, when I think of what I do, I'm like, I'm not that big of a deal. I'm not. I'm blessed that a lot of my friends and family think I am, but I'm not.

But something cool I get to do, is I get to do these cool podcasts and these interviews, and these blog interviews, and these cool Q & As, and these giveaways. And people always ask my advice for entrepreneurs, because if you know my story, you know where I started. Right out of college, I immediately started writing, and writing turned into starting an editing business, which turned into utilizing social media to promote things I wrote. And before you know it, I was like having a full-time client load doing digital media marketing, entirely self-taught.

I went to school for psychology, for crying out loud. And so, that's my backstory. And this started in 2010, and here we are in 2018, and I'm still doing it. I mean, naturally, over the last couple years I've been employed full time, and I've taken a break from the freelance life, and I always come back to it. But I always have my hands-on entrepreneurial projects, most honed explicitly in on marketing and digital media.

Something that I always get asked in interviews or in network groups are questions about social media tips, tactics, and strategy. They want to know the current trend or most popular tool in digital media is. They want to know my biggest, and best secret for being successful is. I'm happy to speak on that, and I can give you advice 'til I'm blue in the face, and I love to share the knowledge, but if I can give one tip to people, regardless of what field you're in, it's to stay current. Stay relevant. And I know that sounds so cliché, but if you don't stay current, you don't stay relevant, you will become stagnant and stale, and your place on the map of whatever industry you are in will cease to exist. Your blueprint within your industry will fade. People will most likely forget you.

Listen, guys, we are in one of the most competitive, fast-paced, overpopulated generations of society there have been. Meaning everyone is going into marketing, everyone's going into finance, everyone's going into healthcare. Everyone is going into everything. The workforce is oversaturated. And that means that we need to do our best, we need to find our "it" factor, as spoken about earlier. We need to hone in on what we're good at, what is going to set us apart. But the second piece to that is to stay current and stay relevant. Here's what I mean. My industry specifically (digital marketing) will change overnight. A trend that was great yesterday could be dead today. I don't know. You never know, you absolutely never know. That's one of the things about it, and it's exciting, but in the same breath, it's exhausting, and it's obnoxious. Because you think you have a handle on social media, you know, as a social media expert and digital media expert, I'm like, "Yes, I've nailed the Facebook ad thing." And then, two days later, I see an article on Verge that the Facebook algorithm has changed yet again, and unless my client has $1,000 a day to drop, they can kiss their social media ad campaign goodbye. It won't do anything. That type of stuff.

You have to stay relevant, and you have to keep current. So part of my job is on a daily basis looking at trends, looking at what's current, I'm looking at what's going on in the world. I make it a point a couple of times a year to go to workshops, seminars, and certification classes and courses, to expand upon what I know. Because what worked in 2010 in my field, and most likely in your area as well, did not work in 2015, and it sure as hell is not going to work in 2018.

And it is so important to continually and continuously brush up on your field of expertise because it's guaranteed that everyone around you is doing the same. It is crucial for you to stay on the radar in your industry, and not go around with a chip on your shoulder because back in 2010 you were a big deal. There are new "big deals" in your field now. You have to reinvent, re-understand, and re-dedicate your time to learning the trends, the tips, and the tactics used to get ahead in your industry.

Now, right now I know I'm speaking primarily to those in marketing, social media, business, things of that nature, but honestly, this applies to anything. I could see this applying to an array of industries, like medicine. We've become so much more advanced in medicine as it changes day by day. People are continually learning. Their knowledge is overflowing, and they're frequently uncovering newfound knowledge.

Another thing is always to update your creative assets. That's another way to stay current. Have the criteria for your resume changed? Update it, even if you're not looking for a job. Just update it, have it ready to go. You never know. Have your LinkedIn refreshed and ready to go. Have a recent profile photo. I'm serious, this all goes into the whole picture, the whole, holistic view of what it means to stay current, stay relevant. Do not have a Facebook profile picture of you in 2013, because I guarantee you, you do not look like you did in 2013. Stay current, stay relevant. Look like you are ever-flowing and fluid and continually making changes, efforts, advances, and excelling and succeeding. That is what staying current and staying relevant does.

Update your blog, updated your Linkedin, your resume, and bio to reflect the most recent info. Have your site updated, have your site mobile-friendly and ready to go.

And make sure that you know everything that is going on in the world. Make sure you are well-versed in pop culture. Make sure you know what's going on in society. You may fucking hate politics, but make sure you at least know the major names on the headlines. If you can go to a news website and understand what they're talking about, you're good. I'm not asking you to look at seven different types of sources and be able to do a direct quote and provide a Washington political correspondent-type response, but just know what's going on around the world. Stay relevant, stay current, because that is part of your "it" factor, and that is what will make you shine. And that is what will push you onward to the next level.

Stay current in life, stay current in your career, and stay current in your growth and self-actualization.

Chapter 24.
Social Media is a Lie

WHEN I STARTED using social media, I immediately figured out that how we look in real life in photos wasn't going to be acceptable. Before you knew it, all these photo software apps started storming through. There was one, I think I've spoken about it, called Picnik, and with one click I was able to have darker skin, and I was able to whiten my teeth, something I would never be able to afford to do at 19 years old, still buying Ramen. Before you knew it, more photo apps came up.

There was the whole air-brushing app. Then there was an app with a feature where within a matter of months you could change the shape of your nose. Let me tell you how thankful I was for that because of my Armenian roots and my Armenian nose. I was so grateful for that.

Originally when all these apps came out back in 2010, and in 2011, and maybe all the way into 2012, I heavily edited my photos on social media. Who didn't? Who remembers the Picnik photos where we would have the neat little writing like "Friends forever, nights like these" and then we'd have some weird sort of stamp or quote that didn't even apply to the photo. And then we would throw on this blue filter and then this border around it, and there we go. Before you knew it, you never really knew what the original photo looked like. And so when all these apps for pictures on social media started, they blew up, and then you look at everyone's profile picture, and it went from being one that was taken at youth group to one that was heavily edited with at least ten different options, and four filters slapped on. It was just a no-brainer, everyone did it.

And before I knew it, I was so obsessed with editing my photos, and then I would upgrade the apps or get the Pro membership and be able to edit the shape of my face. If you want to go ahead and quote chapter 7 to me since not everyone is a photographer, go for it. And looking back, my body image became so skewed. And looking back, when I look at photos of myself during those years, up until the last couple years, I won't lie to you, I've heavily used filters in the past and airbrushing and stuff. It was fun. I was hard on my body. But I look at photos of the past, and I'm like, "Wait. I can't remember. How did I look?" I couldn't tell you how I actually looked back then. Isn't that sad!? I couldn't tell you because those are the photos used to document those years. And I slapped eight filters on there, and I'm pretty sure I did something new with my teeth because I don't think my teeth were that white. And unless I got a nose job without my knowledge, I don't remember my nose looking that cool. And it's so sad to me. And those couple of years ago, that was just the start of it. Now you have an app, you upload your photo, and it edits everything for you. You don't have to go through all the settings. It alters you to look what Hollywood or society would tell you to look like.

As I walk through the streets of Brooklyn and I see these middle schoolers taking selfies, and then immediately after taking it they're like, "Well, let me put a filter on it," which makes me so sad. What a superficial, artificial social environment kids in this generation have to deal with. It's everywhere, and it's impossible to escape it. Snapchat filters that make us a cat, but a cat with a sexy edge to us, and perfect complexion, and a thinner face. This all contributes to poor body image and trying constantly being plugged in on our phone.

I could go on and on about the topic of misleading appearances on social media. Let's talk about the notion that everyone miraculous has their shit together across social media. There are plenty of people in my life who are either shitty people or have some shit going on in their life on the regular. We all have those people. However, if I were to hop on one of their social networks and read their daily—no, hourly posts, I would think they have the best life ever.

I can just hear younger me gushing about people on social media, thinking they've got it together. Oh my God! Their life is perfect. They have a house. They have a couple of acres. They have a great marriage. Their kids are so cute. Look at their Christmas card. It's like a photographer followed them around or something. Oh. And their extended family loves them. I bet their family never fights! My life sucks.

The people I think have it together actually have some of the most messed up lives possible, but social media masks all that. It's a lie. Some of my most favorite moments on social media were some of my worst days. And I know this is true for many of us. We post our highlight reel on social media. We publish the best moments. We post our greatest milestones, our moments that make us feel spectacular. We post ourselves on the days we are not bloated because we're bleeding out of our vagina. We post, and we upload, and we speak the days that we feel our greatest, when really behind the scenes we can be at our lowest.

We can be dealing with the most significant demon. We have no idea what takes place on the other side of the film, of the computer, of the tablet. But social media force us to put our best face on, our best foot forward, our best possible fake mask on and say, "Hello world. This is my highlight reel. How does it compare to yours?"

There are psychological diagnoses being given to children, adolescents, and young adults based on social media. There is Facebook Depression now. It is a thing.

We compare ourselves to other's lives, to other's highlight reels. We miss out on our moments looking at theirs. We airbrush our lives. We airbrush what we're going through. We put on a show so that we are accepted when in reality we accept what is far better than any superficial lie. I find that if I am open and honest, I can provide a more significant influence and greater mentorship. I can meet more people and connect more when I'm raw and honest.

When I came forward about my PTSD last year and my book came out, I cannot believe how many people emailed to message me and were like, "Thank you. Yes. I thought you had it all together. I thought you were perfect, but you're not. You struggle, and I struggle too. And the fact that you struggle, and I struggle, it makes me feel not so alone."

It's not that they weren't happy for me that I was coming out of it. It's not that they were celebrating that I was fucked up too. They were relieved. They felt not so alone because social media force us to lie. And I have found that my most significant moments, across these social media networks, have been the moments that I bared all, emotionally exposed. Transparent, open, and honest. I believe it is only then that you can truly relate to another human being.

We see all these social media influencers and public figures and celebrities on there, and they talk about wanting to make a difference in the world and make a change. And then they continue posting about their perfect lives with their sponsored posts and their beautiful couture gowns. That's not how you change the world. That's not how you influence. That's not how you touch others. You touch others by being honest about the moments that are not your highlight reel.

My point to you is if you're going to go on social media bragging about your life accomplishments, be sure to show that you're normal too so that others don't cut you out because they feel too inadequate compared to you. Just be transparent. Be honest. It'll get you so much further. I know many people in my life who are like, "I don't want the world to know my downfall"—well then, don't be a fake-ass bitch and only post your highlights. It's not all rose-colored glasses or nothing. Either be real, be genuine, or just don't post at all.

Social media has been utilized for some great things but has also brought so many demons into our lives. So I encourage you with everything you post, ask yourself, "is this a true representation of who I am?". I find a lot of times that social media strategists like myself try to curate inapplicable content to attract followers, yet in the process, we turn off our current followers. Don't post things that will annoy your current network to grow your network. Make sure that you find that beautiful balance between maintaining your follower base and attracting new followers.

And also, when you post about yourself, is it truthful? Is it genuine? Do you look like that? Does it look like you have a nose job? And a reminder, in case this book has taught you nothing so far: as you scroll through people's Facebook feeds, what you see is not real. It is the highlight reels. It is the best moments. It is not the outtakes; it is not the bloopers, it is not real life. Cut yourself some slack; you're doing great. Be you. Be yourself. Love yourself, and realize that everyone else is on a path and a different journey. And what's on their timeline (on both social media and IRL) does not depict your schedule and your journey for your own life.

Chapter 25.
Cut the Cord

I KNOW THIS SOUNDS like such a harsh phrase, and quite honestly, it is—it's fucking brutal—but it's so important. Along the way in life, you will create connections. Those links will be friendships, relationships, encounters, and spiritual bonds. That cord may get a little snug around you and maybe a little bit too tight, and it may not work anymore. That, my friend, is what we call a growing of people, experiences, and things in life. That is called growth, and it's a positive thing. What's cool is sometimes, the cord, the metaphorical cord—I love to speak in analogies and metaphors—sometimes, this metaphorical rope will stretch with you, and it will grow with you. It will bind with you and bounce back and be a part of your journey and the fluidity of your movement. And, there are other cords that are stuck. They don't let you go anywhere. They constrict, they confine, and they drain. Those are the ones you need to cut.

Over the last ten years, I have had to snip many cords. Some of them I genuinely miss, but for some of them, my life was made better the day I did it. You don't just wake up one day and say, I'm going to cut the cord with so-and-so, and it's time to cut the cord. It doesn't work that way; you don't just wake up one day and decide this is going to happen. There is a string of events that lead to it, such as something this person did or something you did, and it starts to create tension on that cord. Perhaps you said or did something, and they were afraid to express their disappointment or their sadness or how upset they were, so they swallowed it, and the tension started. Or maybe they said or did something, and you're stewing about it, and you've been boiling about it for years, and that creates tension on the cord.

Then you swallow, and you hold it in and hold it in, and the more you do that, the more resentful you get. Then you get to a point when you cannot fucking take it anymore, and you have two choices. You either explode and will likely sever the friendship, or you can talk it out. You may also continue ignoring it, but that usually goes in one of two ways. Often, because we hold all this in, we hold in all these offenses, these grudges or these issues and we don't use our voice because we're afraid, we're not taught to use our voice. We're more likely to have a blow-up or a falling out because we never used our voice in the first place. How many times can you think of a childhood friend, and you ask your other friend, like, "What happened to so-and-so?" And they'll be like, "Oh we had a falling out, or we're not friends anymore." You sit there puzzled, like, "You guys were the dream team. What happened?"

Most likely, they had to cut the cord, and there are many reasons for why you cut the cord. Some of them are justified, but some of them are sadly not. Some of them just happen over time, some of them are abrupt. Before you lean in that direction, however, I ask you to consider—is this a person you want to be without? Can this be resolved through an awkward conversation, leading to resolution? It's incredible what can happen when you sit down with someone and say, "Hey, I noticed there's some tension. Do you have five minutes to talk it out?" And then explain what you are feeling. It can instantly make the friendship better.

Last year, a very close friend of mine and I we were in the middle of a tiff and were honestly at a crossroads. It could have gone one of two ways, but we both valued our friendship enough to say, "Hey, can we talk over lunch break and iron everything out?" And you know what? I had a pit in my stomach that day. I had lost my appetite, and my hands were cold. I was so nervous to meet with her, but once I did and we talked it out, we were able to iron out the unsettling moments of resentment and settle the tension; this little cold war was over. Ultimately, we were able to move forward. Had we not done that, I think it would have festered. We are both very passionate, strong women with strong backgrounds, so I also think it could have backfired and severed the friendship completely. Sometimes words don't work, as sometimes the person isn't willing to hear what you have to say or vice versa. I was blessed to have someone mature enough who valued our friendship enough that she didn't want to have to cut a cord, either.

If you are in a toxic friendship or relationship I spoke on earlier, and you do need to cut cords, bear in mind that there will always be another cord, there will always be new connections, and there will always be new friendships. And there are two different ways to cut the cord. One way is to explain. I don't think there's a right or wrong in how to cut a cord, but delivery is critical. You can either explain and sit someone down, saying something like, "I love you so much, but this bothered me, and I've been waiting for it to change, and I've dropped hints for your behavior and your patterns to change, but this is still hurting my feelings. And hey, I try to live a life that's healthier and more mindful and better for me, and this particular friendship is dragging me down because of x, y, z." Then you pose to them the question, and you make them have the control and say, "Do you think this is something we can work through?" And then the ball is in their court.

After explaining why you're cutting a cord, and they may just say, "You know what? I think we've outgrown each other," or "No, I'm not willing to change," or "Fuck you"—and then you'll at least know you tried. You tried. The other way, which I'm noticing seems to work very well with girlfriends, because sometimes we just outgrow each other, and sometimes it doesn't require an explanation or a five-page letter writing in milky pens. Sometimes we just drift away, and sometimes we just need to cut those cords. Sometimes we just need to distance ourselves from one another slowly. I notice this is sometimes healthier for people, when you're dealing with a friend or family member who has extreme emotions, rather than it get into a huge heated blow-up, you'll start drifting away.

You're allowed to do that; you're allowed to prune your plant. You're allowed to prune your tree of life. You're allowed to let people go. You're not a bad person for it. If it's what you need right now, if it's going to make your life less stressful, then that's what you need to do.

A great gauge of this is if you see someone's name on your phone and when you're stomach sinks, or you're like, "Yuuuccck," and you get that ick factor, it may be time to cut a cord or at least reevaluate the friendship. Sometimes it doesn't require that long, drawn-out conversation. Sometimes you can just slowly drift away. You can take a little longer to reply, you can conveniently be busy all the time. You can let it slip away, and eventually, they will get the hint, and they'll realize that the time has come to go separate ways and that this doesn't have to cause hard feelings. It is possible. You are allowed to cut cords. You're allowed to cut cords with friends. While it's often complicated and I hope that this is the last resort, remember you are allowed to cut the cord with truly toxic family members. Toxicity is toxicity.

I saved this one for last—are you ready? Have you cut cords with your exes? Oh, girl, I know where this is going. You're going to read this, and you're going to tell me the exception, that you're the exception. I'm here to tell you that you're not; you cannot be friends with an ex. If you had any level of intimacy with an ex, then I don't personally believe that they should be in your life. There's a reason why there is movie upon movie and song upon song about people who are unable to just stay friends with their exes. They end up falling in love and having wild crazy passionate sex, and then the movie ends without them living happily ever after. If you had any intimate connection, you should not be friends with your ex.

If you were meant to stay friends with exes, then society wouldn't have created the multimillion-dollar rom-com movie genre. This entire genre is devoted to stories where you're able to remain friends with your ex, but then it backfires, and you fall in love. It's just not natural; it's not normal. I'm begging you -- cut the cords you need to cut. Maybe it's a friend from high school who you've been trying to stay friends with because everyone on social media is friends with them. Perhaps it's your ex-boyfriend, and you're staying in their lives because you're afraid that they're going to do something stupid if you walk away. Maybe it's a sibling who is toxic for you right now, and seeing their name on your phone makes you want to be sick because of something they did or said.

You're allowed to cut that cord. You're allowed to do that. It doesn't mean it's permanent, but if it's going to make your life easier and better for it, you're allowed to sever those ties. Growth happens. People change. People leave. People grow. People explore. People succeed. People come back around. This is a beautiful circle of life. You do not necessarily have to keep every cord since birth intact. It is not a mandatory thing to maintain every single friendship and connection you've had from the get-go.

Give yourself permission to do a spring cleaning of those in your life who no longer serve you. Permit yourself to cut cords when needed. Give yourself permission to step away from someone who is toxic. Give yourself permission and allow yourself to take a step in a different direction. Sit in the quiet and ask yourself -- who needs to be weeded out from your life? What cords can you snip and most importantly, who are the ones you want to move forward with on this journey we call life?

Chapter 26.
You Don't Owe Anyone
an Explanation

OKAY, DESPITE THE fact that you think you owe someone an explanation, I'm here to tell you: you don't.

I know, I know, I know. It doesn't fit with how we've been raised. I mean, think about it. From the moment we can talk and make any decision as a child, we have to tell our parents why we have to explain. We have to explain why we think we deserve to go to that football game or why we deserve to have our curfew extended. And that's all fine when you're a child, but then this crazy thing happens when you hit adulthood, and you don't have to owe anyone an explanation anymore.

You don't owe anyone an explanation of the 5 W's in your everyday life. The who, the what, the where, the when, and the why. Since the beginning of time, we've had to give explanations. It was a survival technique. We were growing; we were changing, we were not adults. But then as you hit adulthood, we start feeling this crazy O-word, and it's called obligation.

Obligation sucks. It creeps in. It is a guilt trip; it is a crazy guilt trip of a ride, and it causes us to do things like say yes to plans when we don't want to do them in the first place. Obligation causes us to sleep with someone because he or she paid for a nice steak dinner. Obligation causes you to explain to your colleague the 18 billion reasons why you need to take a mental health day. You don't owe anyone an explanation. You don't owe anyone an apology for anything you do unless you are within the realms of mandatory responsibility, in which it's then about your job, your education, or the law. I think that's going to be my safety blanket here.

I first started learning this concept last year when I was starting to get my life and my stress levels under control. You know, even as an adult, with your family, you don't owe anyone an explanation. You don't owe anyone an apology—whether it's family, friends, what have you—for why you choose to date someone. You don't owe anyone an explanation if you decide not to go to that concert. You don't owe anyone an explanation if you choose to get a seventh tattoo.

It's about what do you want. What are you looking for? What will be in your—I love the phrase—"highest good." What will bring you to your best version of yourself? What will allow you to achieve your optimal happiness and a sense of balance? Find it, and then do that. And you don't need to explain it to anyone along the way.

Dude, you're an adult. You're making it in this adult world. You're making it. You're living. You got it. You don't owe anyone an explanation. Unless your parents are paying for your rent and everything you eat and drink, you don't owe them an apology. They're your parents. Your job is to respect them. But it's not necessary to explain every decision you make and action you take.

I want to shake my friends and colleagues and just be like, "No, listen, you don't owe anyone an explanation." But then I'm reminded that I am still struggling with this. I am still struggling with this on a day-to-day basis, and so I sit quietly and I offer myself as a support and I guide them along the way with little nuggets of information, but I don't dare do a metaphorical shakedown and tell them to try to knock some sense into them because I am still struggling with it too. And if you remember, one of the things I strive to do if I'm struggling with it is to not preach on it; and if I've pushed through it, I will guide you best I can.

So know that as you're reading this, I'm struggling with this too. I'm struggling with the fact that I don't need to send a paragraph explaining why I can't make an event. Instead, I will select all that I have written in my iMessage app I will backspace, and I will say, "I'm sorry, I'm not able to make it, but I hope you have a great time." And leave it. All you owe is an RSVP.

As you adopt this mindset, you will find you are stressed less; you are less anxious, because the only person you have to hold accountable, and who you owe an explanation to, is your inner self, you.

But if you're not religious, it's just you. You talk to yourself. If you're cool with it, then it's cool. It's good. Release yourself from the expectation that you owe an explanation. Listen to that again. Release yourself from the expectation that you owe people an explanation. You don't owe them anything. You don't owe anybody anything.

We live in this guilt trip of a world, a guilt trip of a society where everything is guilt and obligatorily driven, and as a result, we are drained, we are exhausted, we are anxious, we are depressed, we feel less than, we are depleted, because we spend our life trying to be good and be accepted in other people's eyes. My love, you don't owe anyone anything. Every explanation's optional, and it's not encouraged.

So you'll find that as you do this, you will feel freer, you'll feel more liberated, you will feel more at peace. And it takes practice. Again, I am still struggling with it. It is a habit to be broken. I struggle with it all the time. But the more I do it, the more comfortable I'm getting at it.

And here's the other cool thing about not owing anyone an explanation. As you decide to water down and streamline those that even get an explanation, you'll find that the people that aren't cool with the fact that you're not giving an explanation peace out on their own. Anyone that's not okay with self-growth and self-development, with a skill set such as this, this not feeling obligated to explain yourself and fall all over yourself, they will peace out. They won't feel like for whatever reason, they may get offended, they may feel unimportant, they may feel like you've taken a step back.

So you'll be doing yourself a favor not owing anyone an explanation because the people that are not genuinely in your life looking for you to have a stress-free, healthy, mentally sound life full of clarity and growth and self-actualization, they won't stick around. I have a couple of friends that I've stopped falling all over myself explaining and stopped kissing ass with and they've just vanished into thin air over the last couple months. And at first I was scratching my head going, "What changed?" And oh, I stopped falling all over myself because of guilt and obligation.

Release yourself from the expectation that you owe an explanation, and as you do, you will feel freer, you will feel lighter, and you will start loving yourself more. Because you know, the only person you owe an explanation to is you. And you should explain to yourself, "Am I happy? Am I healthy? Am I whole? Am I working towards my work in progress? Have I achieved my goals? What can I do to make myself feel better? What can I do to make my situation better?" Have that dialogue with yourself. That's the type of explanation and explaining you should be giving. The only person that deserves an explanation is you.

Chapter 27.
It's Quality Over Quantity

YOU'VE HEARD THIS expression, I'm sure, since you were a little wee one, yes I said wee. But I've learned it's true more and more the older I get. The further I get in my career, the more people I meet, just the more mature I become, it truly is quality over quantity, and I mean this in many different aspects of life. But I'm speaking specifically to people in your life.

I used to be the person that would obsess over her Facebook friends count and her MySpace count, and sit there and do eeny, meeny, moe to pick who would be my top friend because I had so many friends. I didn't want to offend anybody, but…I was obsessed. I would sit there with my AIM, AOL Instant Messenger window open and I would just stare and wait for people to come online.

That was me in the early 2000s. And I would just have random superficial conversations with people. But

I didn't care because it was quantity. It was as many friends...I got this weird-ass like, high, overseeing how many times my bottom Windows 98, shit, maybe it was even Windows XP footer bar lit up because that meant that I was having all these conversations and I was so excited. And I would get high. I would spend hours. I mean, no wonder I was so chunky, I didn't move because I was having all these conversations.

With MySpace, I was obsessed. I would just, you know, make sure I have the maximum amount of top friends possible on MySpace so that everyone could see that I had so many friends. I couldn't just pick four or five or six top friends on MySpace. I had to do a ton.

When Facebook became the forefront of the social media evolution, I was so obsessed with having all these Facebook friends. Hell, now I have like 4.6 thousand on my page. I don't know who the fuck 4.3 thousand of those are, to be quite honest with you. Because when Facebook started, what did I do? I had to have the quantity. I had to have a ton of friends. I would add random-ass people in Ohio, who were absolute nobodies that I had no idea who they were, just to have friends. I would, this is embarrassing, but I'm going to tell you how obsessed I was with having quantity over quality.

I would search Tumblr, I had Tumblr, who doesn't still have a Tumblr, let's talk about this, but I would search Tumblr for the hashtag #facebookfriend, and I would look for people to Facebook friend. And then

I would look for people to follow. I was obsessed with quantity.

Now, it's paid off a little bit, with what I do. Naturally the more subscribers, you know, as many of you know, my first book became even a blip on the radar because I had a bunch of Tumblr followers who followed my journey when I was engaged to a military man and blah, blah, blah. We're not going to talk about that this chapter or in this book if at all possible. But that's how I gained my following.

So, quantity is excellent if you're trying to be a social media influencer and are speaking to that particular brand. But I'm talking about the number of friends and people in your life and all the noise, noise, noise. I'm trying to give you a backstory of how obsessed I was with the quantity and the numbers.

When Facebook Messenger Chat, whatever the hell it's called, started, oh my God. Like, message window after message window, just mindless conversations. "Hi, what are you doing?" "Not much, how are you?" "Good. What are you doing?" "Oh just eating lunch, blah, blah, blah." Just stupid...but it was quantity; it kept me distracted from what was going on in my life.

And then when texting happened, when I was, you know, finally off the track phone situation, raise your hand a little louder for the people in the back if you remember the track phone days, where you had to pay for every text you sent, and it was off your card, the monthly card that you either got or your parents would get you if you begged them. And you got unlimited texting? Oh, it was all over. It was all over after that.

I would constantly be texting. I would have 32 conversations going at once. Window after window after window. Then I got the iPhone. Oh, I should have been locked up. I should have been put away for how addicted I was to my phone. Because it was conversations. It was quantity. And I would brag about it. I was such a little shit, you know, into college. "Yeah, I have to respond to my 17 conversations." It was just all about quantity for me; it was not about the quality.

And it wasn't until I moved to New York that it really hit me how important quantity was because when I left Michigan, I left tons of friends. I left maybe 50 people, I mean, 50 people that I would consider "close friends." Because that's how many people I was constantly in contact with. It was draining, and it was exhausting. I love them wholeheartedly, and I've always loved them to this day, but I entertained too many friendships at one time, and I didn't spend enough time on them.

And maybe that's hard to understand or hard to digest, but perhaps many of you understand what I'm saying. There was so much white noise, and it wasn't until I moved to New York City, because, newsflash, when you move to a new city with a one-way ticket, and you do not know a soul, you have no friends, so your quantity is zero. Your quality is non-existent because your quantity is zero. I had to start from the ground up, and I tried to make friends very quickly right off the bat once I moved here, because I was yearning for those coffee dates, oh I want a booked schedule, I want all these friends. Let me tell you something, women on the East Coast, in New York; they don't have time to be your friend; they don't. I mean, let's talk about it. There's even the Bumble app with a Bumble BFF because you don't have time to connect with people and so there's an app that, while you're dating, you know on your dating app, online dating, you can also switch it over and look for a friend. Like, that is how hard they are to come by.

And so, I'm searching for this quantity. I want my new posse; I want my new list of 50 people that I can hang out with at any point. Fourteen months went by when I was in New York when I did not have one friend. I had acquaintances. I had people that asked how my lunch break was. I had no friends. And, it was really lonely. But, I want to offer a major shout-out to what we call the Babes of 4L. As I write this, we all love each other very much, and we're sisters at heart. But, it's interesting to see that even though we have this bond, as I'm watching things unfold, everyone is about to go down a different path.

These girls, these Babes of 4L, became my best friends. It's a group of four girls, and I only met them because I lived with them. I do not doubt in my mind that had I not been, for lack of a better word, forced to live with these people, I wouldn't have made these best friends. And, while these girls were not my quantity, they were my quality.

It's hard to say, yeah, my best friend, well yeah, I have like, I have four friends out here, and that's it. It was different. It was different for me, but I learned to appreciate, and I've been in New York nearly four years and obviously I've been blessed to meet people and I have some great friends, I have some people I would call acquaintances, I have some people I would call good friends, and I've added a bestie or two to my little repertoire, my little posse. At the end of the day, it's that sisterhood. It's that quality over quantity and these girls; we were together nearly every day.

I had to work on the quality of these friendships. It was weekend trips together; it was sitting there with our heart to hearts. It was having that one person to call when you were, you know, you had the shits, and you had no one else to call, and you called them. And these relationships were built on quality. They were quality, good friendships. We built each other up, and we love each other, and we are the sisterhood. Even if our life gets too busy and too crazy, I know I could pick up the phone and dial any one of these girls, these Babes of 4L, and my quality friendships will shine through, and they will be there for me.

That was the first time I learned that it's about quality, not quantity. I also am learning that this is becoming a part of our growing and our evolution; becoming who we're meant to be as adults. I'm noticing everyone in my friend group that once had 50 people, the girl that was a girl in my hometown, the guy that was the once quarterback of his high school team and got a scholarship, the one that had 80 people surrounding him at a party, is down to a couple of friends.

I'm finding that the older you get, it's going to matter about your core. It's going to matter about that quality. So as you see this happening, I urge you, I encourage you, not to fight it, not to resist it. If you notice that some cords are cut, to reference our last chapter, if you notice that your little friendship circle is maybe dwindling, fear not. It's okay; it's just going to teach you to appreciate the ones you do have. This is a natural part of growing up. It's not about the quantity anymore. It's not about how many Facebook friends you have, in real life or metaphorically on social media.

It's not about who are your "top friends" are or your Snapchat score. It's about the quality of those people who have chosen to have you in their life purposefully and intentionally, and it's about the caliber and the special people that you chose to have in your core and close to you. So embrace the quality, and dim the lights on the spotlight of the importance that we once placed on quantity.

Chapter 28.
Not Everyone Is Going
to Like You

SOME PEOPLE ARE going to hate your guts. Okay, I know the main thing throughout this whole book is that I'm super raw and honest and it's probably bruised your ego a little bit. Since we're near the end of the book and you're still standing, I'm just going to keep going, okay?

Here's the thing. People are going to hate your guts. I mean, people are just going to genuinely not like you. You're going to try your absolute damnedest to make sure that they like you. You're probably going to fall all over yourself at some point in your life and make yourself look like an absolute idiot. People may just not like you. And there are several reasons why, which we'll get into in a sec. But, it just really sucks that sometimes, no matter what you do, people don't like you.

This came into play, my first encounter with this notion when I was in high school, and I went to a very, very small Christian school, and there were a handful of girls that were in the high school portion of the school. I mean, a handful of girls I could count on maybe two hands and a half of a foot how many girls were in my 9th through 12th grades. Some of them, no matter what I did, just did not like me. I mean, I, granted, was a homeschool transplant, so I already had the whole Cady Heron from "Mean Girls" thing going on. You know, that stigmatism that I was weird because I was homeschooled.

But I tried. Dude, I tried. I did the whole Aeropostale thing, then they all went for the Abercrombie thing because, you know, we want a moose embroidery emblem over our non-existent bras instead of the Aeropostale butterfly. So then I started doing the Abercrombie thing; I did it too, and I listened to all the music that they did. Rest assured, I tried to do my makeup the way they did. I even ate the same lunches they did. Do you think I wanted hot pockets? You think I wanted hot pockets? I was lactose intolerant, but I fucking ate those hot pockets anyway. I wanted to fit in so bad; I just wanted them to like me.

And then, you know, Ms. Innocent, Cady Heron 2.0 at my school, I didn't know a damn thing about sex. I didn't know anything about boys. I didn't have my first boyfriend until I was 16. And so then, they started talking sex and you know, making out and what base they went to. And I'm still thinking that they're talking about a baseball team that our small school didn't even have, and they're really talking about sex.

I'm like, "Oh yeah, I know what you're talking about, kidding, I don't." Google on our little pay-as-you-go track phones was not a thing. So then they started reading Cosmopolitan Magazine, and I was like, "Oh yeah, I read that all the time too." So I bring a copy to school, and I'm like, trying to look like I'm an avid reader. Like, "I have a subscription to this bitch," and "I do not." I was just so discouraged one day because no matter what I did, they did not seem…a couple of them, in particular, just did not seem to like me.

And I came home one day to my mom, and I'm like, "What the fuck?" I didn't say "What the fuck," because I would have gotten my mouth washed out with soap and cayenne pepper and then probably spanked with a wooden spoon because that's the Armenian way to discipline your children, spanking them with a wooden spoon, but that's neither here nor there.

I was like, "Mom, what the hell?" And she said, "Hope, Hopey." Yes, my mom called me Hopey. "Not everyone's going to like you, and there's nothing you can do about it." My mom is good at giving advice. Sometimes, my mom is very blunt, like the time that I was in ice skating for a couple of years, and I wasn't excelling. I really stayed at the same level for over a year, and then she finally just told me that I wasn't going to be in the Olympics, and I would never be Michelle Kwan or Nancy Kerrigan, and I should probably hang it up.

So this was one of those moments when she's like, "Not everyone is going to like you, and there's not anything that you can do about it." That was harsh. That was hard to hear, but she's right. She's absolutely right. You can try everything in the book, and someone still might not like you, and you're like, what is it? Is it me? Well, clearly, it is you. It is you. I mean, it's their problem, and it's probably their loss. Unless you're a terrible person or you smell funny, it's probably their loss, but not everyone's going to like you. And, there are a couple of reasons for why that is. But, the number one reason I would say is that personalities clash. You know, type A's and type B's—they can either coexist or get really annoyed with each other because type B just wants to Netflix and chill, and type A wants to go a mile a minute. Other times, the oldest child may be too strong-willed and not get along with the middle child. Sometimes, two different personalities—I think there's something with algebra, like, you know, a positive and a positive make a negative or a minus or some weird math thing. Hi to my math teacher, who is hopefully not reading this.

Anyways, sometimes two strong personalities just repel each other. And sometimes, two chill personalities—well, probably nothing's ever said. They're quiet, but they may not get along well either. There's a special formula for what makes a good friendship, a good partnership, a good employee-to-employer relationship, a good peer-to-peer relationship. But, sometimes, it does not work, and you just have to accept it. It's probably them; it's probably something they're working through; it's probably something you have no idea about.

But then there are people who just do not like you. So stop trying so hard. Stop trying so goddamn hard. Stop kissing up. Stop trying to relate. Stop, don't be a chameleon, don't walk into a room and try to assume the persona of everyone around you. Not everyone's going to like you, so don't try so goddamn hard.

I want you to think about it. Do you like everyone you've ever come in contact with? Let's just have a real talk for a minute. How many times do you just not like someone? You'll talk to your best friend about them, and you'll be like, "I don't know, I just don't like them." And your best friend will question you, and of course, counter it because of course if you don't like someone they're not going to like someone. It's what a good best friend does. I'm kidding, calm down.

I don't know, you know, what your response is, "I just don't like them." It happens. Not everyone likes chocolate; not everyone likes vanilla. Not everyone likes Brussels sprouts; not everyone likes ice cream. Everyone's not for everyone. So stop wasting your energy trying to be liked, stop wasting your energy trying to be accepted. You are enough, and not everyone's going to like you, but you know what? I'm willing to bet there's a bunch of people that do. So stop trying so hard in the lunchroom. Stop looking like an idiot who's trying to schmooze their way at a conference during the meet and greet mixer time.

One of my worst pet peeves is when I'm at a conference, and you watch these women weasel their way to each table to try to be included in that particular table. They want to be liked by everyone. They want to leave the conference with a list of 200 attendees and all their social media info just so they can have more contacts. Most of us can see right through that. Stop trying so hard. You look like an idiot. Just let your friends, your peers, your people gravitate to you and don't force it. Okay? As I said, chances are you don't like everyone either.

Not everyone's going to like you. Some people are just going to fucking hate your guts, and you just have to move on with it, accept what is, be the best version of yourself, and put your time and energy into the relationships that matter instead of trying to please, impress, and be accepted and appreciated by everyone around you. You'll be waiting a long-ass time.

Chapter 29.
Stop Being So Readily Available

WHEN I FIRST met my current boyfriend, he started out as a very good friend of mine. From the get-go, I always admired the random lessons and nuggets of information he would give to me and teach me, and I would still take them with so much value. This lesson, in particular, was entirely out of the blue and unexpected. We were out to lunch once, and my phones – yes, I said phones – were beeping incessantly. "Do you need to take that?" he asked. "No, I'm good." Chirp, chirp, chirp. Beep, beep. A Twitter noise, a Gmail, an Outlook noise, a Skype noise, an iMessage noise, a Facebook notification noise, a WhatsApp noise, and a Snapchat noise, always on the hour.

I started feeling like a twitch because I wasn't responding to them right away. I was trying so hard to impress him because I was very impressed that this particular friend, now my boyfriend, was able to just set his phone in his coat pocket and leave it. A crazy notion. He's psychotic. "You sure you don't need to get that?" he asked, noticing and feeling me tense up, and I continued to look towards my phone. "Well, if you don't mind," I said. Oh, I thought to myself. He's giving permission, for lack of a better word, for me to check my phone as I always did.

I responded to the plethora of messages, replied to a comment on Facebook, got back to my mom, to let my little brother know I would get in touch with him later, told my best friend I'd call her this weekend. And of course, while I was at it, I had to check my Instagram Direct messages and my emails. I set the phone back down. There I went again. I picked it up. Well, he said yes the first time. Just might as well check it again, and I proceeded to do that. I proceeded to do that for this lunch meeting, the next one, dinner. And then one day, he just looked at me, and he's like, "Oh you know, you don't have to respond right away, right?"

I looked at him like he was speaking French. "Yeah, I do," I said. "Why? They'll be there later." Okay, this guy was psycho, and it was never going to work out between us because I have to be readily available. "I'm always readily available," I explained to him. "I mean, I have my phone on my ringer all night so that all the notifications come in. If anyone needs to call me, they can reach me, or they text me. I've always been this way. My friends know that I'm always on call. My family knows that I'm always readily available." "Well that can't be healthy," he shot back. I just looked at him like, "Who the hell do you think you are?"

He's like, "You don't have to be so readily available. You don't have to respond right away. They're not going anywhere. If it's an emergency, their text will be followed by a call or five. You don't need to respond to everyone." Now, I'm going to tell you a little secret. I'm still really struggling with this. I'm still working on this, but he was right, and I've been working on it in the last year, and the times that I (1) put my phone on silent or Do Not Disturb for a set amount of time or (2) notice on my Apple watch that I have a text but don't get back to it until later, I feel so much more relaxed and at peace, which you would think would be the opposite, right?

You think because you have it pending and it's right there, you have to respond to it right away, and if you don't respond to it, you'll get anxiety. That still happens to me. But, I've been working on this and training myself. Habits that we try to break are very much like muscles. If they're out of shape, we will feel some soreness, resistance, or tension. I am working on this muscle. That is me learning the art of not being so readily available. But, the times that I do that and set my phone down, don't check it right away, or don't feel like I need to respond, I'm so much calmer.

Another lesson my boyfriend taught me during our courting stages, when I think he was just trying to impart all of his awesome knowledge to me, is the fact that even if you do read someone's message or listen to someone's voicemail, you don't have to respond and react right away. You respond and react at a time that works for you. What I highly recommend doing when you get a text from someone is if you want to respond, great. But if you respond within a minute, guess who's going to expect a response to their next text or message within a minute as well.

And before you know it, you've taken up 25 minutes of your morning that you had already scheduled out to catch up on emails just to respond back and forth to these texts, because you what? You feel like you owe an explanation. Hello, Chapter 26. You don't owe anyone an explanation. So, it's very important to exercise this. It's going to take some time, but you will feel so much more relaxed. Did you know—and I'm learning this too—did you know you don't have to respond to clients right away? I mean, I think they say the kosher thing to do is within 24 hours on a business day and a weekend.

You don't even have to fucking respond unless that's written in the contract. Did you know that? Because I've just now learned this last year. I truly have been working on this with myself. Even if I'm holding my work phone, I have been working on the fact I don't need to respond to clients right away. I continually use the phrase in this chapter that I am working on it. I don't want to sit here today and write to you a 10,000-word chapter on how to stop being so readily available, when I'm working on it myself.

Know that I'm struggling with this just as much as you, but I'm learning it as an important lesson that I need to learn and as a muscle I need to exercise. You do not need to be readily available to clients unless it's a client emergency, which should be spelled out before you start working with any client or any employer. You do not need to be on your work phone all the time. You do not need to respond to their email right away. You do not need to answer their IM unless you are on the clock working in front of your computer and their response is needed. Set boundaries. This goes back to setting boundaries. Chapter 20 speaks to setting boundaries and to taking care of yourself.

Chapter 18, be selfish. Adopt that self-care. You don't need to respond right away. This has to do with clients. This has to do with friends. Stop being the friend who, the moment someone hits send, your chat bubbles appear to them, okay? Unless you want to be sitting there on your phone all day, you are wasting your time, energy, light, and love to be sitting on your phone responding to people all day. I could spend all day responding to people, and I would still not get through all my messages between Facebook and Instagram and Twitter and myself and my text and my emails. I couldn't. I'm learning the art of delegating a set time to respond to everyone,

And if I do choose to respond to someone, not having to have this constant communication tennis where it's constantly served back-and-forth nonstop. Let some time go by. Let's text someone, set your phone down, and come back to it in a couple of hours. If you read their message, and you're not looking for a constant, continual communicational conversation, then respond, set your phone down, and a couple of hours later, respond. In time, they will learn, and they will pick up the hint. So, if your friends are used to you responding within a minute, and then you slowly start dragging this out where you respond in two hours or three hours or four hours, they will come to expect that of you, just as they expect you to respond quickly now.

The same applies to family, to clients, to colleagues, and in your dating life. Don't be the girl that responds instantly. I'm not talking about playing games. Make no mistake here. I'm not talking about playing games. If you're in a relationship, or you're dating someone, and you want to speak to them constantly, God bless you. However, don't be that girl who, when you start dating someone, responds immediately because you are setting the tone for the duration of this dating span, whether it be a couple of days, a couple weeks, a couple of months, a couple of years. So, set those expectations now. No one likes the person who hops on their phone and responds at the moment you hit send.

So I encourage you to stop being so readily available. Take some time in between. Do not be absorbed with the obligation. They owe an explanation, and in this case, this explanation is responding immediately. You will find that as you do this, you will have more time. You will be more productive. You won't feel like you're in a mental fog because you're not constantly poked into your phone, and you will feel not as suffocated and overwhelmed. Remember, I'm working on this lesson with you. So, I completely understand that it can be difficult to get the hang of it, but I know that just like any muscle in our body, we can exercise this one too.

Chapter 30.
You're Failing If You're
Not Even Trying

WE LIVE SO many years of our life in fear. Scared of being loved, scared of being accepted. Most importantly, we're scared to fail. Here's the thing: You're failing if you're not even trying. I realize that this is a phrase that is plastered all over Pinterest, and more importantly--most importantly--it's easier said than done. I get it. Really.

May 29, 2014. Our family's lives changed forever. My sister and I were hosting a brunch for our expectant best friend, and we got a call, and our lives were forever changed. Our little brother had been the apple of our eye, our little prince, the little shit. Able-bodied, handsome, talented, had his world ahead of him, he could have been anybody, anything in the world, he could have had anyone. He lit up a room just by walking into it. Whenever met a stranger, he walked away with a smile on his face, a new conversation had been had, and a new friend in his world. He smiled from the moment he was a baby. We wondered what was wrong with him because all he did was stay quiet and smile. He was the light of our lives.

And he was nearly taken from us on May 29, 2014. We got a call that my brother had been in a motorbike accident and was paralyzed waist down. We didn't know much, other than he was turning blue and it didn't look like he was going make it. My sister and I immediately did what we do best, and we pushed through adversity. And we pushed through all the doubts in our minds and the fears, and we arrived at the hospital in what seems, looking back now, like a flash of light. The flick of an eye.

I don't know where you stand on your faith or beliefs, so I always try to be sensitive so this part of the story. Hell, I am still trying to figure out where I stand on the faith piece myself. But what I do know, is that on that day, we had a supernatural and omnipotent present leading us through. It led us through the darkest hours. My brother's faith was also so incredibly strong so I know that coupled with the faith of our entire community, pulled my brother through. We sat there waiting, as our brother was at death's door. Somehow, he pushed through.

I still don't remember at what point it changed and it all turned around. I don't remember what made this go from what seemed like a horror story to the potential of having a happy ending. To start this horror story, the doctor came out, and he told us he was sorry, but our brother would never walk again. He said he was permanently paralyzed from the waist down, and there was no chance my brother would ever be out of a wheelchair.

I remember gripping my waiting room hospital chair and sobbing as if someone had died. I then remember lowering myself to the ground and weeping. I wept for his legs. I wept for the fact that my brother wanted to be a basketball player. I wept for the fact that my brother had the world at his fingertips and hadn't even... he was just a sophomore in high school. He had the world, and this was taken from him.

I mourned his ability to walk. I mourned the fact that we would be taking care of someone in a wheelchair, and I remember sitting there mourning the happy family everyone knew us to be. I don't remember anything else; I've blocked so much of it. What I do know is that after that conversation, a life-changing conversation was had with my brother.

The neurosurgeon walked into his room, expressed his condolences as if someone had died and said my brother would never walk again. He let my brother know this, and he apologized. Not an ounce of sympathy on this man's face. And my brother looked at him with determination. He didn't say anything. His mouth was clenched shut; he was in too much pain, and he could barely keep his eyes open. But something switched in my brother that day. The fire was lit back into his eyes. The passion was brought back into his heart. And while he didn't know what he'd begun, he'd begun to try.

He tried because he decided to continue to live, day after day. He decided to push his way out of the ER. He and my mom decided to push for some of the best rehabs in the country. Between him and my mother, they pushed with the insurance company, with many different medical supply companies, to be able to give him the medical tools and the equipment he needs, and the therapy he needs and the wellness techniques he needs.

My brother, though he still uses a wheelchair, is now walking with braces, and at this point, as we head into 2018, my brother can feel from the waist down. Only because my brother tried. Only because my brother pushed through. Had he not tried, he would have failed.

And he continues to work, and he continues to try, day after day after day. And so no matter what he does, no matter how much progress he makes, he will have never failed, because he's always tried. He tries every day. He tries when he decides to get out of bed and transfer himself into the wheelchair. He tries when he makes the choice to eat and replenish his body with nutrients. He tries when he drives to his rehab program after his 13-credit hour week at school.

In the annual checkup my brother had on the anniversary of his accident, he went to the neurosurgeon. At this point, he was able to hold himself up without a back brace. He had just been fitted for braces to be able to walk using a walker, and he wheeled in there, and he told his doctor, "You should never tell someone that they can't do something. You should never limit them like that. Can you imagine, sir, what would have happened to me had I not tried anyway? I would've still been in this chair, without any core muscles, with zero recoveries, because I would've believed you. Had I not tried, who knows where I could have been?"

Damn, Luke, drop that goddamn mic.

I use that lesson for many people, including myself, every single day. Had Luke not pushed that envelope, had Luke not tried, he most likely would not have regained the recovery he has, and he would not be as far along as he is today. It is because he tried, knowing full well that he may fail, that he can succeed.

I think we do this often all throughout our lives. We're so afraid to fail that we don't push the envelope. We don't even try. We're so afraid to fail that we don't even start that new fitness plan and that new eating plan, and as a result, we don't ever get anywhere. We're so afraid to fail at a new job, because we hate our job. We're looking for a new job, but we're so scared that we don't even apply to the one that could be our dream job because we may get rejected for it.

We're scared to fail, so we don't start our passion project. We don't start a side business because what if we fail? You're failing by not trying. Doing something, anything, the slightest thing that benefits the future you—and the future you could be the tomorrow you, the next-week you, the next-month you, the next-year you—anything that benefits the future you is a step in the right direction; it cannot be marked as a failure.

You're failing if you are not trying. You're failing if you do not take a step in the right direction towards a better you. You are failing if you do nothing. That sounded very Yoda-ish, I know. But, it's so true. Failure is marked by being stagnant and complacent. Failure to most means an unsuccessful attempt at something. I believe this to be untrue.

If you try anything, if you work towards anything, if you hit any goal or work towards any goal, you are building momentum. You are trying your hardest. You are working towards something, and that, my friend, is not to be ever taken as a failure.

Some of the best things I've ever done in my life are because I took steps forward even when I was afraid. I was so afraid of failure, and this continues to be my biggest phobia. I have a fear of blood work, and I have a fear of failure. That's it. I don't fear death; I don't fear heights; I don't fear spiders, I think they're kinda cool. Especially the little ones that jump. But failure? Failure scares the absolute shit out of me.

Fear paralyzes me. Yet, I need to take a step in the right direction, every single day, towards a better version of myself to break that paralyzing fear of failure. If I can do it, if Luke can do it, you can do it too. It's not done overnight, though; it's absolutely done in baby steps. It is a conscious decision day after day after day.

There's a way to get there. Write out your goals, write out your dreams, write out your ambitions. If you're not a writer, type them up on an iPhone note. If you're not an iPhone person, and you have an Android, I'm sure there's some weird-ass note app you can use to write this down too. If you don't wanna write it down, just think about it. Manifest it. What can you do for your future self? And what can you do today, tomorrow, a week away, a month away, a year away, five years away, that will help build that dream and will help allow you to succeed and give you a better life? One that's mentally sound, healthy, and just all over more positive?

What can you do for the future you? Figure that out, and then do something about it. Maybe it's editing your resume today, even a page of it. Try eating healthier today, and not having that extra set of carbs. Consider the notion of mending a bond with a loved one whom you miss. If you do something today for the future you, and do something every day, you are well on your way to winning at life. Success begins with a mindset. Creating a healthy mindset is a muscle you must strengthen and that's done by doing it day after day. So by picking one thing each day for the future you, you are well on your way to creating a new habit and toning that positivity muscle.

You're more likely to die of failed goals and lost ambitions and dreams if you do nothing. That's most of the world. Most of the world suffers through their nine-to-five staring at the clock. So, my love, do something. Get up and do something. Don't sit in paralyzing fear for the risk that it may not turn out the way you have it in your grandiose head. You fail if you don't try. By trying, you're ultimately already succeeding.